CAMBRIDGE
Primary Science

Workbook 1

Jon Board & Alan Cross

CAMBRIDGE
UNIVERSITY PRESS

Shaftesbury Road, Cambridge CB2 8EA, United Kingdom

One Liberty Plaza, 20th Floor, New York, NY 10006, USA

477 Williamstown Road, Port Melbourne, VIC 3207, Australia

314–321, 3rd Floor, Plot 3, Splendor Forum, Jasola District Centre,
New Delhi – 110025, India

103 Penang Road, #05–06/07, Visioncrest Commercial, Singapore 238467

Cambridge University Press & Assessment is part of the University of Cambridge.

It furthers the University's mission by disseminating knowledge in the pursuit of education, learning and research at the highest international levels of excellence.

www.cambridge.org
Information on this title: www.cambridge.org/9781108742733

© Cambridge University Press & Assessment 2021

This publication is in copyright. Subject to statutory exception and to the provisions of relevant collective licensing agreements, no reproduction of any part may take place without the written permission of Cambridge University Press & Assessment.

First published 2014
Second edition 2021

20 19 18 17 16 15

Printed in the Netherlands by Wilco BV

A catalogue record for this publication is available from the British Library

ISBN   978-1-108-74273-3   Paperback with Digital Access (1 Year)

Cambridge University Press & Assessment has no responsibility for the persistence or accuracy of URLs for external or third-party internet websites referred to in this publication, and does not guarantee that any content on such websites is, or will remain, accurate or appropriate. Information regarding prices, travel timetables, and other factual information given in this work is correct at the time of first printing but Cambridge University Press & Assessment does not guarantee the accuracy of such information thereafter.

The exercises in this Workbook have been written to cover the Biology, Chemistry, Physics, Earth and Space and any approriate Thinking and Working Scientifically learning objectives from the Cambridge Primary Science curriculum framework (0097). Some Thinking and Working Scientifically learning objectives and the Science in Context learning objectives have not been covered in this Workbook.

....

NOTICE TO TEACHERS IN THE UK
It is illegal to reproduce any part of this work in material form (including photocopying and electronic storage) except under the following circumstances:
(i)   where you are abiding by a licence granted to your school or institution by the Copyright Licensing Agency;
(ii) where no such licence exists, or where you wish to exceed the terms of a licence, and you have gained the written permission of Cambridge University Press & Assessment;
(iii) where you are allowed to reproduce without permission under the provisions of Chapter 3 of the Copyright, Designs and Patents Act 1988, which covers, for example, the reproduction of short passages within certain types of educational anthology and reproduction for the purposes of setting examination questions.

Contents

1 Living things

1.1 Animals and plants alive! — 2
1.2 Parts of a plant — 5
1.3 Plants and light — 8
1.4 Plants need water — 11

2 Sound

2.1 Sound sources — 15
2.2 Loud and quiet — 18
2.3 Sound moves — 21

3 Materials in my world

3.1 Different materials — 23
3.2 Properties of materials — 26
3.3 Sorting materials — 31
3.4 Changing materials — 34

4 The Earth

4.1 Planet Earth — 37
4.2 Heat and light from the Sun — 40
4.3 Rocks — 44
4.4 Soil — 47

Contents

5 Humans

5.1	Our bodies	50
5.2	Our amazing senses	54
5.3	Similar and different	58
5.4	Staying alive	61

6 Forces

6.1	Moving things	64
6.2	Push and pull forces	67
6.3	Making things move	71
6.4	Floating and sinking	74
6.5	Magnets can pull	77

How to use this book

This workbook provides questions for you to practise what you have learned in class. There is a topic to match each topic in your Learner's Book. Each topic contains the following sections:

Focus: these questions help you to master the basics ⟶

Focus

1. Draw lines from the labels to the correct recycling bins.

Practice: these questions help you to become more confident in using what you have learned ⟶

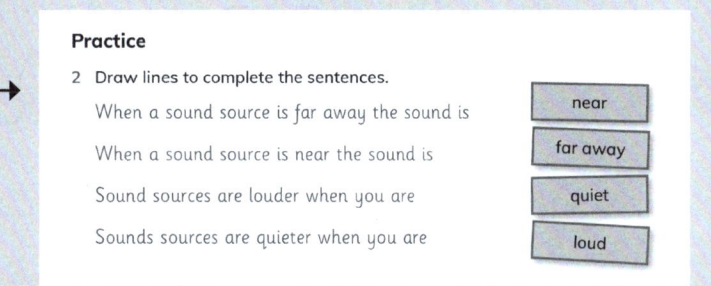

Practice

2. Draw lines to complete the sentences.

   When a sound source is far away the sound is

   When a sound source is near the sound is

   Sound sources are louder when you are

   Sounds sources are quieter when you are

   near

   far away

   quiet

   loud

Challenge: these questions will make you think more deeply ⟶

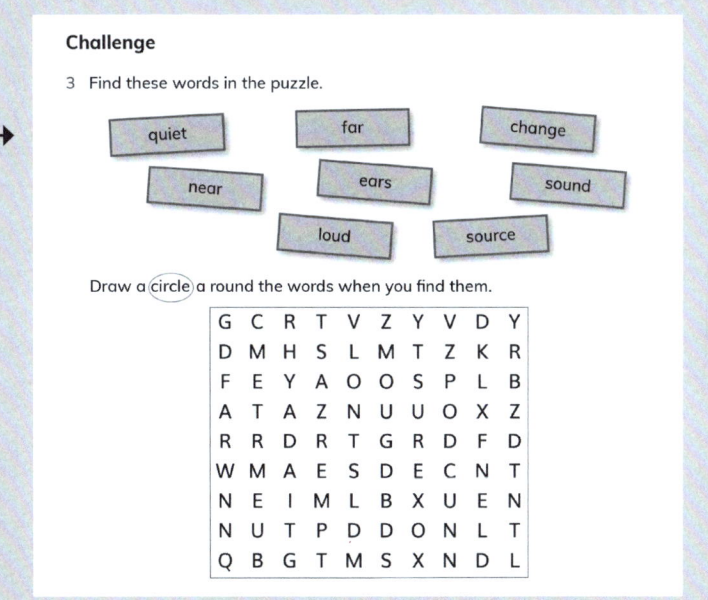

Challenge

3. Find these words in the puzzle.

   quiet   far   change
   near   ears   sound
   loud   source

   Draw a (circle) a round the words when you find them.

G	C	R	T	V	Z	Y	V	D	Y
D	M	H	S	L	M	T	Z	K	R
F	E	Y	A	O	O	S	P	L	B
A	T	A	Z	N	U	U	O	X	Z
R	R	D	R	T	G	R	D	F	D
W	M	A	E	S	D	E	C	N	T
N	E	I	M	L	B	X	U	E	N
N	U	T	P	D	D	O	N	L	T
Q	B	G	T	M	S	X	N	D	L

1 Living things

> 1.1 Animals and plants alive!

Focus

1 Colour in **only** the things that are alive.

1.1 Animals and plants alive!

Practice

2 Draw lines from these things to the right group.

lion   Sun   tree

Non-living   Living

water   butterfly   chair

1 Living things

Challenge

3 Cross out (~~cross out~~) the wrong word in the sentences below.
   Example: A ball is ~~alive~~ / not alive.

   A fish is **alive** / **not alive**.   A cat is **alive** / **not alive**.

   A rock is **alive** / **not alive**.   Water does not need **move** / **food**.

   A cat can **move** / **food**.   Water is **alive** / **not alive**.

4 Write two sentences about this living thing.
   Use some of these words.

The	tree	is	big.
	leaves	are	small.
			tall.

   _____

   _____

> 1.2 Parts of a plant

Focus

1 Draw lines from these words to label this picture of a plant.

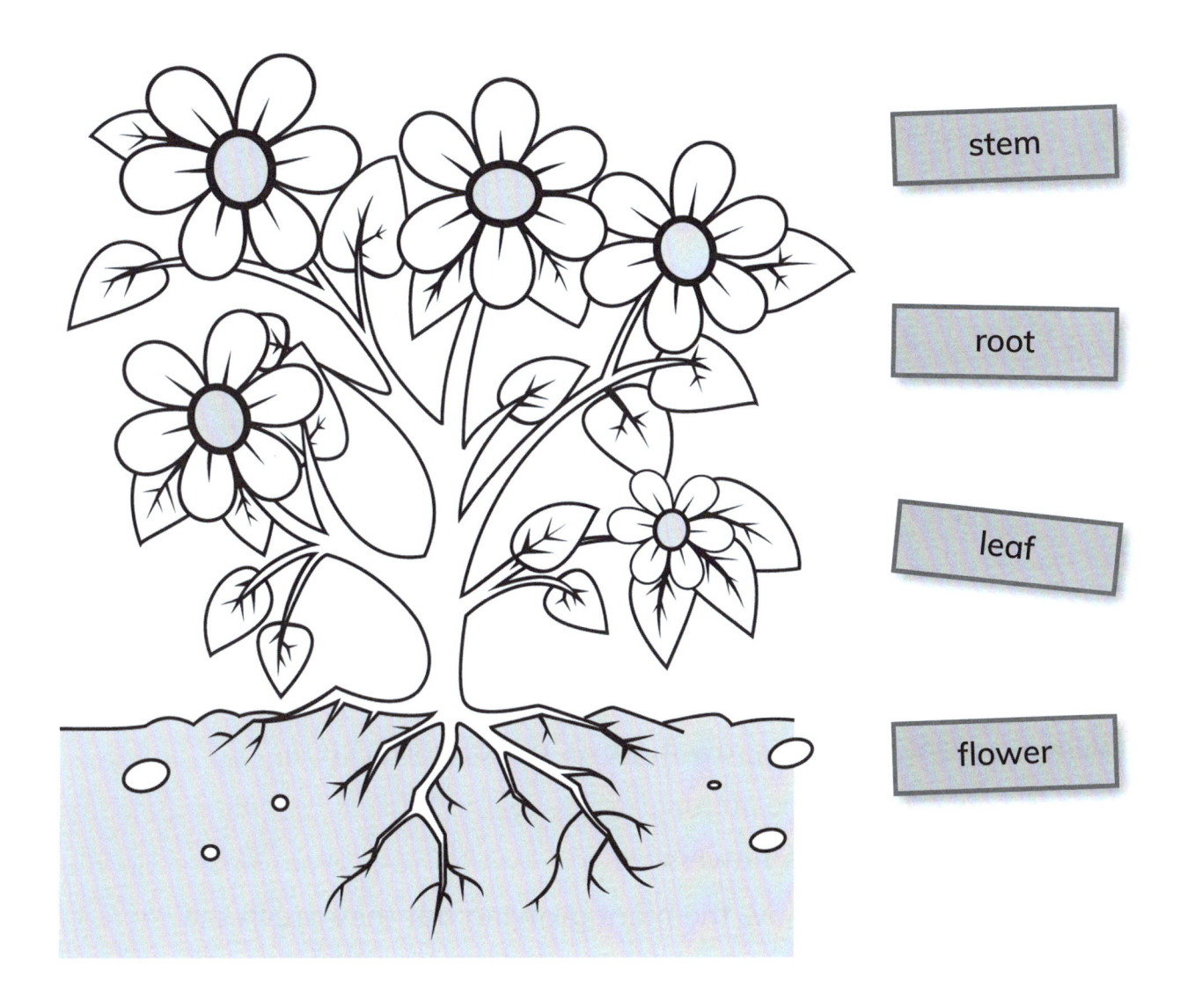

stem

root

leaf

flower

Look at lots of plants. Look at the different shaped leaves and flowers.

1 Living things

Practice

2 Draw lines from the words to each picture to label the roots, stem, leaf and flower.

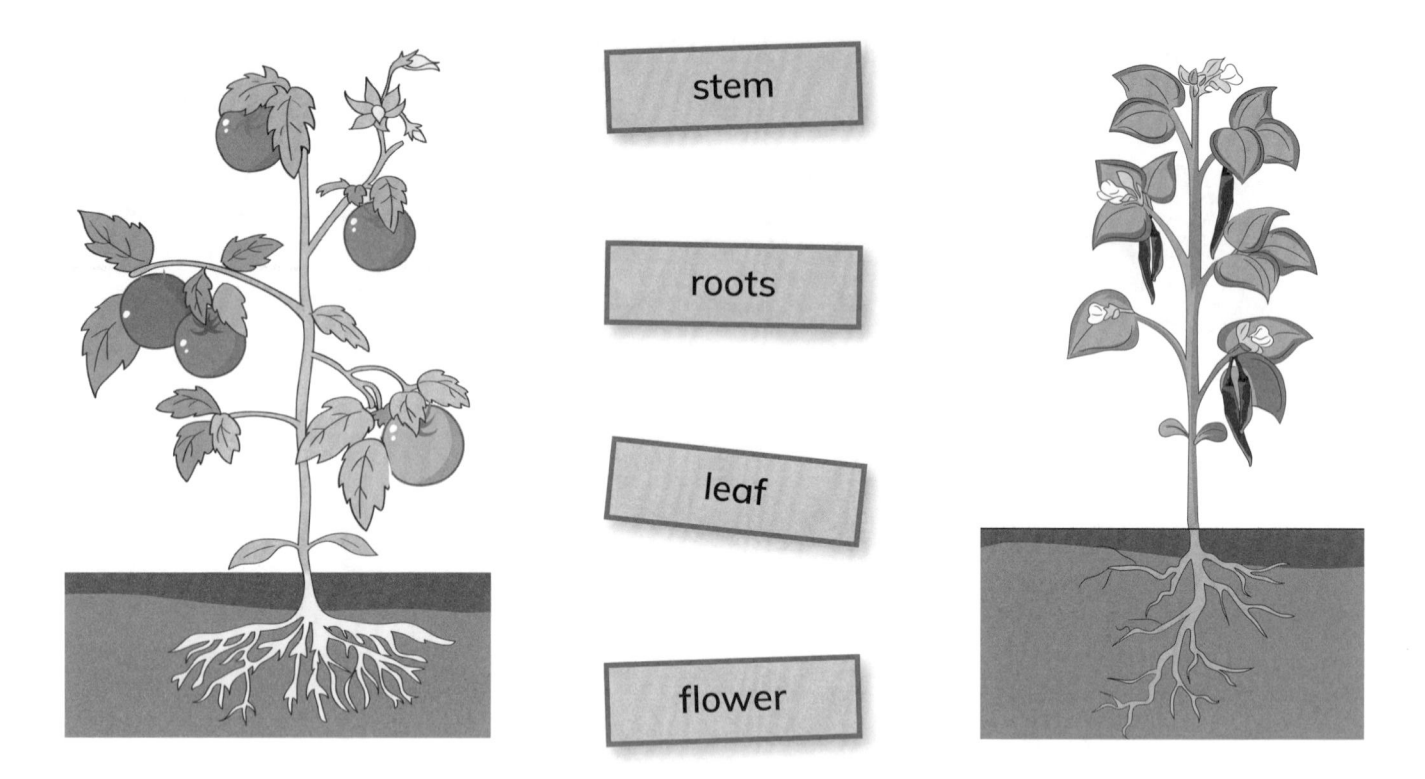

stem

roots

leaf

flower

Challenge

3 When a plant starts to grow it grows a root and a stem.

The leaves grow on the stem.

Later, the plant makes flowers.

These four pictures show the plant growing but they are in the wrong order.

Put the plants in the right order using the numbers in the pictures.

Write the numbers here: _____

1.2 Parts of a plant

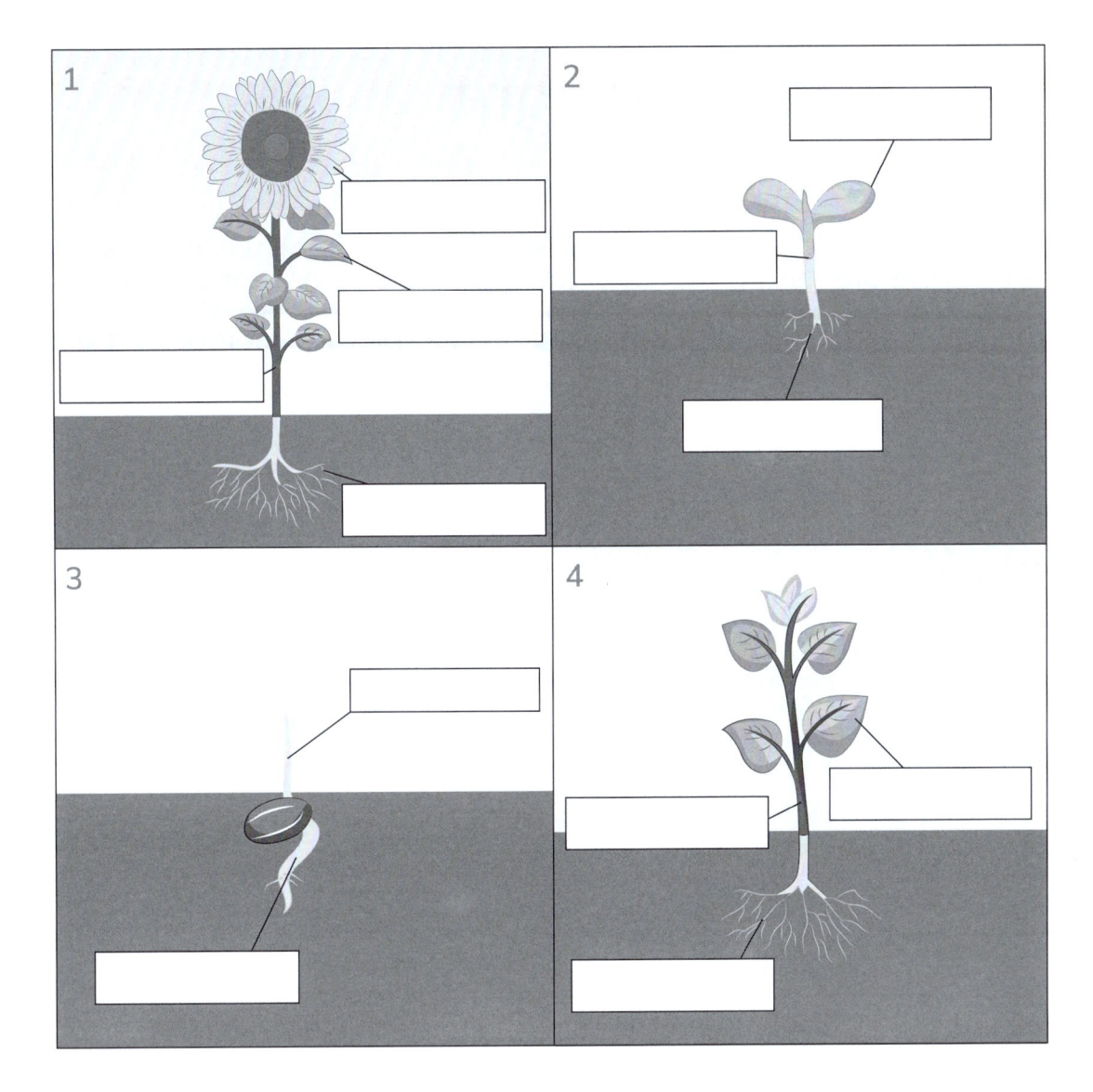

Label the root, stem, leaf, flower in each picture.

4 Put a cross (✗) next to the wrong sentences below:

   a There is only a flower on picture 1 because:
      ☐ the flowers have fallen off in the other pictures
      ☐ flowers are the last thing to grow

   b There is a root and stem in each picture because:
      ☐ you can't draw a picture without them
      ☐ the roots grow first, then the stem.

7

1 Living things

> 1.3 Plants and light

Focus

1 One of these plants is growing in the dark. The other is growing in the light.
   Write the word 'Dark' or 'Light' under each picture. Colour in the plants.

Practice

2 Write the words in the right box.

small leaves   big leaves   tall stem

Plants with light

_____

_____

_____

Plants in the dark

_____

_____

_____

short stem   green leaves   yellow leaves

1 Living things

Challenge

3 Cross out (~~cross out~~) the wrong words in these sentences.

Plant A was grown in the **light / dark**.

Plant B has **small / big** leaves.

Plant B has a **tall / small** stem.

Plant B was grown in the **light / dark**.

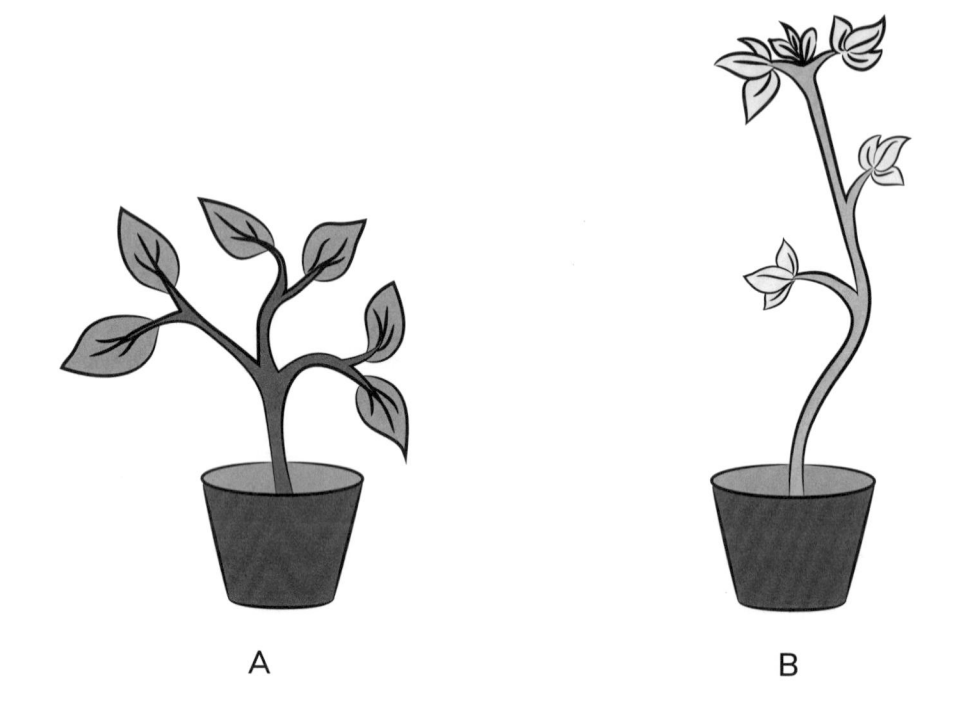

4 Write what you think will happen to a plant with no leaves.

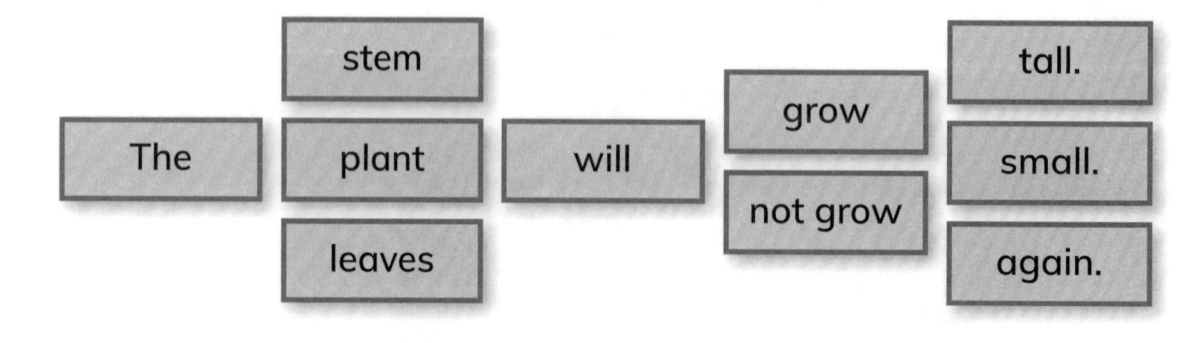

The | stem / plant / leaves | will | grow / not grow | tall. / small. / again.

> 1.4 Plants need water

Focus

1 Look at this plant.

   This plant has no water.

   The plant isn't given water for a week.

   What will the plant look like next week without water?

   Draw a picture of the plant without water.

   The plant is given water. What would it look like?

   Draw the plant after it has had water.

1 Living things

Practice

2 Draw the three missing pictures for days 3, 5 and 6.

Day	Rain?	
1	Rain	(healthy flowering plant)
2	No rain	(wilting plant)
3	No rain	
4	Rain	(healthy flowering plant)
5	No rain	
6	No rain	

1.4 Plants need water

Challenge

3 Look at these six pictures. They show a plant as it grows.
When we stop watering the plant wilts.
The bricks next to the plant show how high it has grown.

On days 5 and 6 we stop watering.

What happens when we stop watering?

When we stop watering, the plant _____.

Colour in the bricks on days 2–6 to show the height of the plants.

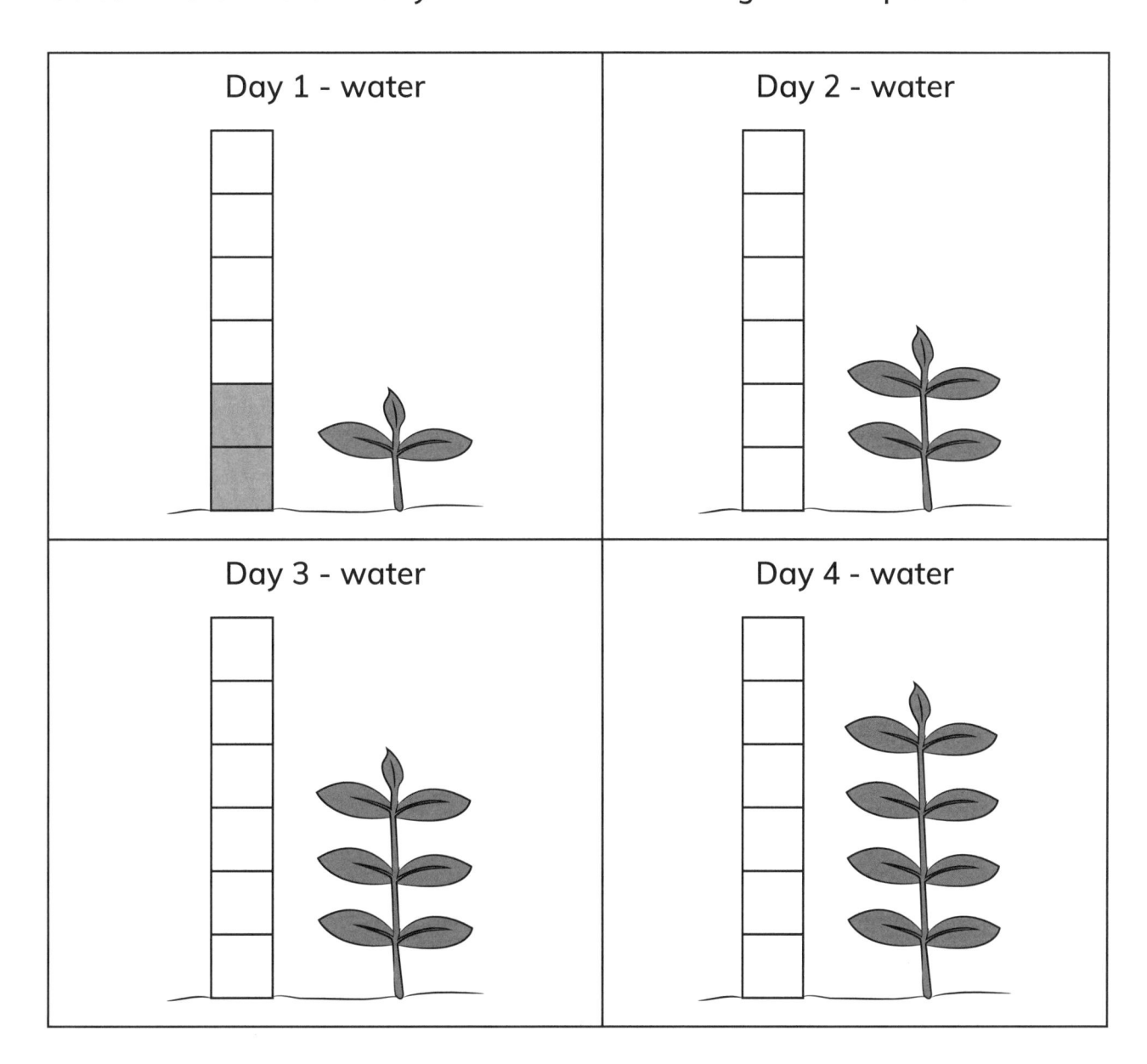

| Day 1 - water | Day 2 - water |
| Day 3 - water | Day 4 - water |

13

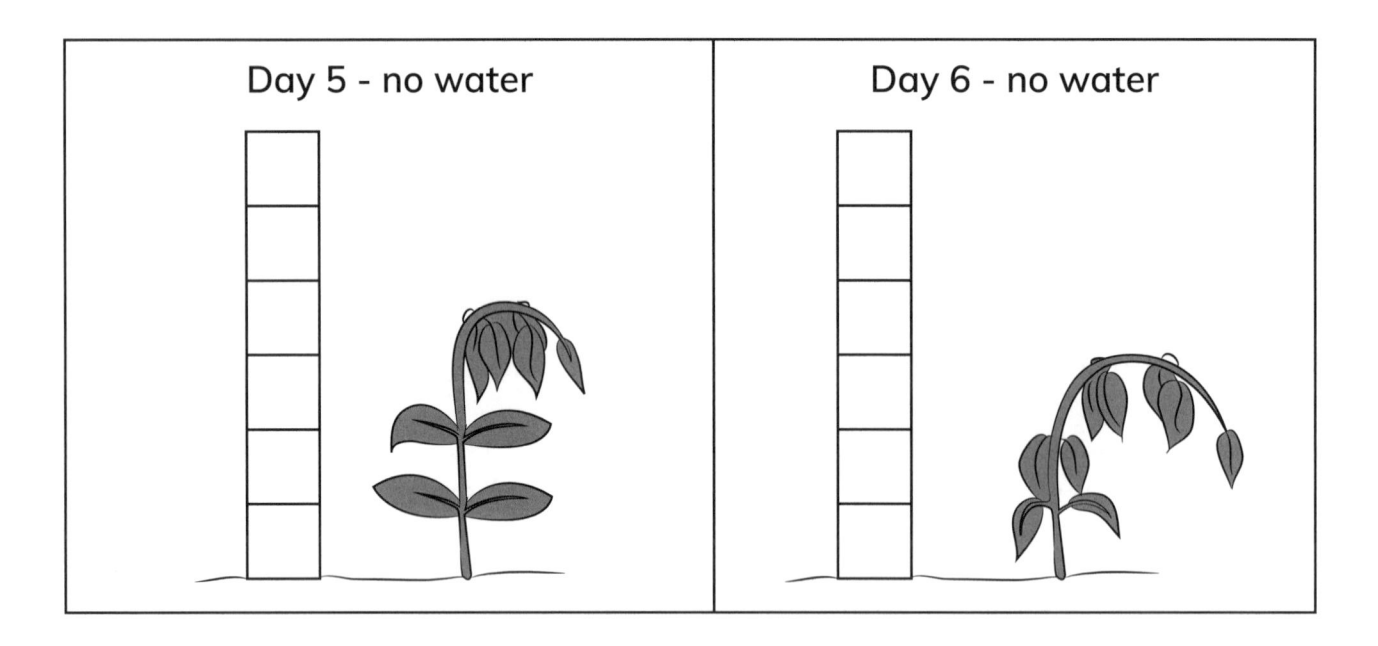

1 Living things

Day 5 - no water

Day 6 - no water

What happens to the height of the plant on day 5 and day 6?

On day 5 the height of the plant was _____ bricks.

On day 6 the height of the plant was _____ bricks.

Why does this happen?

The plant _____ because it had no _____

2 Sound

> 2.1 Sound sources

Focus

1 There are many sources of sound.

   Look at the picture.

   Draw a (circle) around each thing that is a sound source.

2 Sound

Practice

2. There are sounds that you like.

   There are sounds that you don't like.

   On the left side, draw things that make nice sounds.

   On the right side, draw things that make sounds that are not nice.

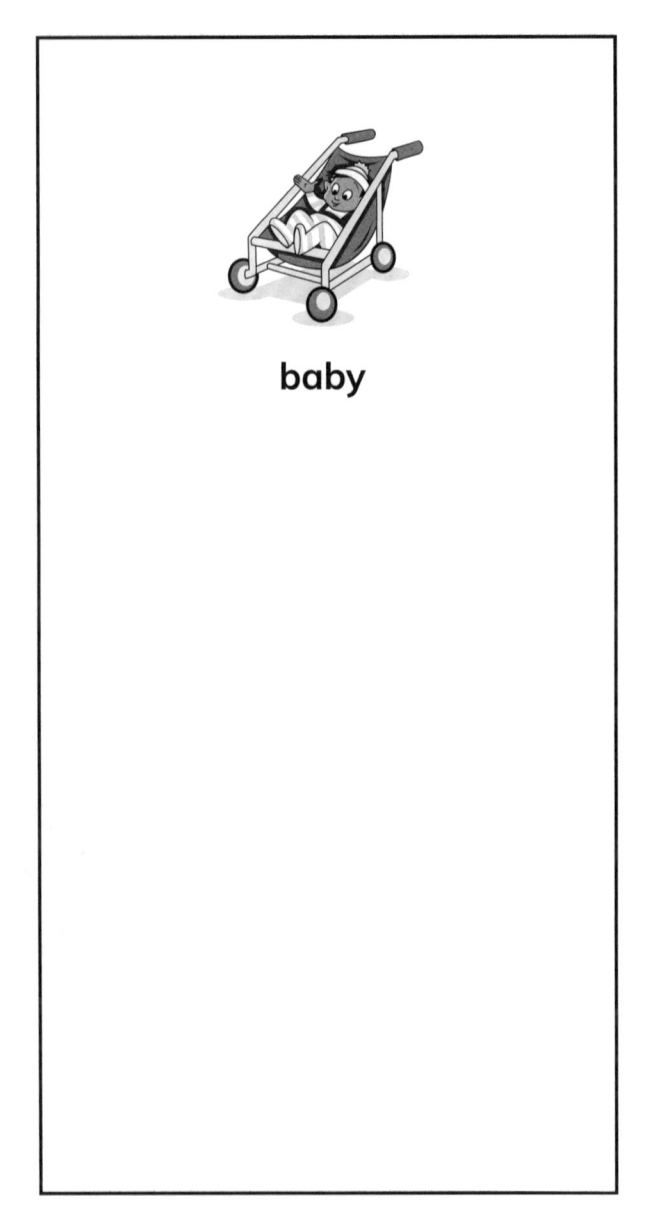

baby	thunder

   Sources of nice sounds | Sources of sounds that are not nice

2.1 Sound sources

Challenge

3   Some sound sources can only be found indoors.

   Some sound sources can only be found outdoors.

   Some sound sources can be found indoors and outdoors.

   Put these sounds into the right place.

   Draw a line from each picture to the right place.

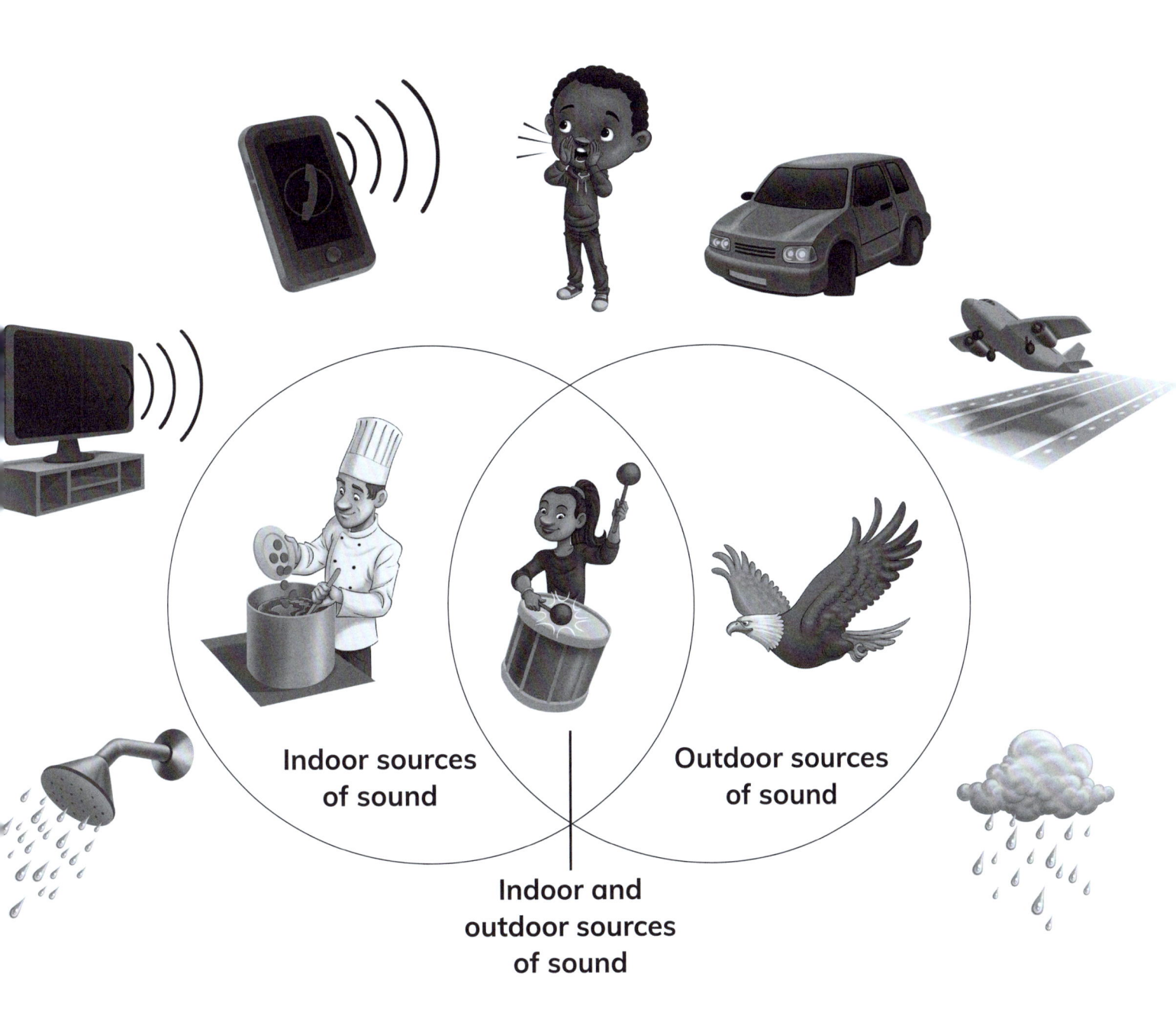

Indoor sources of sound

Outdoor sources of sound

Indoor and outdoor sources of sound

17

2 Sound

> 2.2 Loud and quiet

Focus

1 Look at these pictures.

Draw a (circle) around the correct word to describe the type of sound the sound source makes.

loud / quiet

loud / quiet

loud / quiet

loud / quiet

loud / quiet

loud / quiet

18

2.2 Loud and quiet

Practice

2   Draw these things in the right box below.

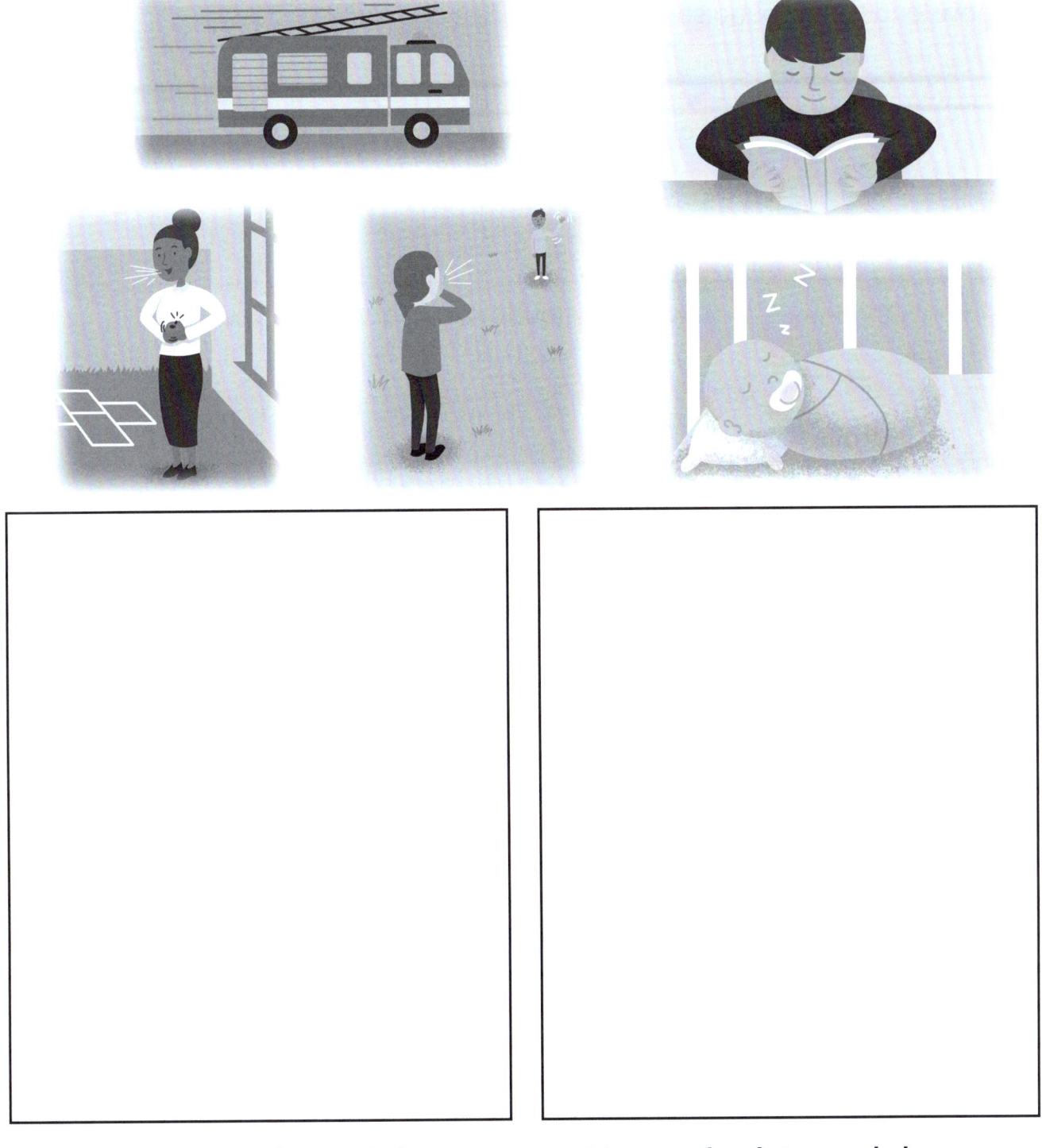

You need loud sounds here   **You need quiet sounds here**

2 Sound

Challenge

3 Look at the pictures. Decide which is the loudest thing and which is the quietest thing. Draw a circle around the word that describes how loud these sound sources are.

Source of sound	How loud is the source?
volcano	quietest / loudest / quiet / loud / very quiet
train	quietest / loudest / quiet / loud / very quiet
curtains	quietest / loudest / quiet / loud / very quiet
tap dripping	quietest / loudest / quiet / loud / very quiet
tap with lots of water coming out	quietest / loudest / quiet / loud / very quiet

> 2.3 Sound moves

Focus

1 Loud sounds can hurt your ears.

   (Circle) only the people who are being safe.

2 Sound

Practice

2 Draw lines to complete the sentences.

When a sound source is far away the sound is

When a sound source is near the sound is

Sound sources are louder when you are

Sounds sources are quieter when you are

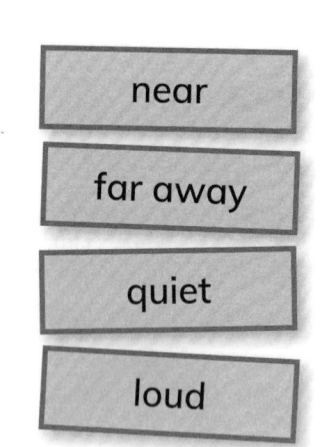

- near
- far away
- quiet
- loud

Challenge

3 Find these words in the puzzle.

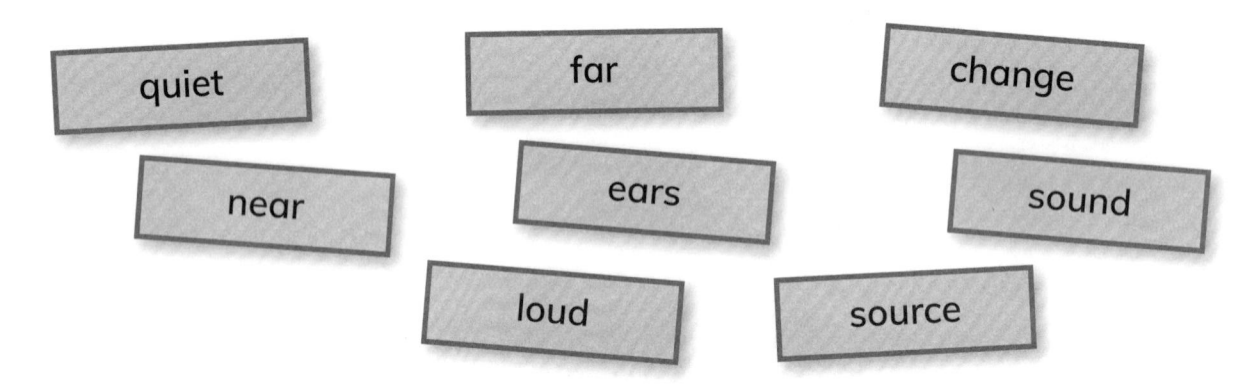

- quiet
- far
- change
- near
- ears
- sound
- loud
- source

Draw a circle around the words when you find them.

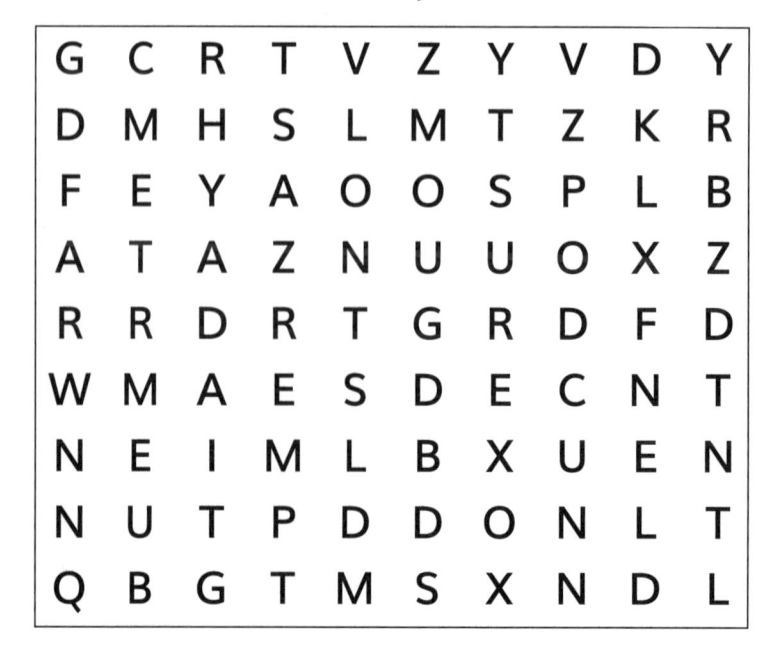

G	C	R	T	V	Z	Y	V	D	Y
D	M	H	S	L	M	T	Z	K	R
F	E	Y	A	O	O	S	P	L	B
A	T	A	Z	N	U	U	O	X	Z
R	R	D	R	T	G	R	D	F	D
W	M	A	E	S	D	E	C	N	T
N	E	I	M	L	B	X	U	E	N
N	U	T	P	D	D	O	N	L	T
Q	B	G	T	M	S	X	N	D	L

3 Materials in my world

> 3.1 Different materials

Focus

1 Draw lines to match the pictures with the materials.
   One has been done for you.

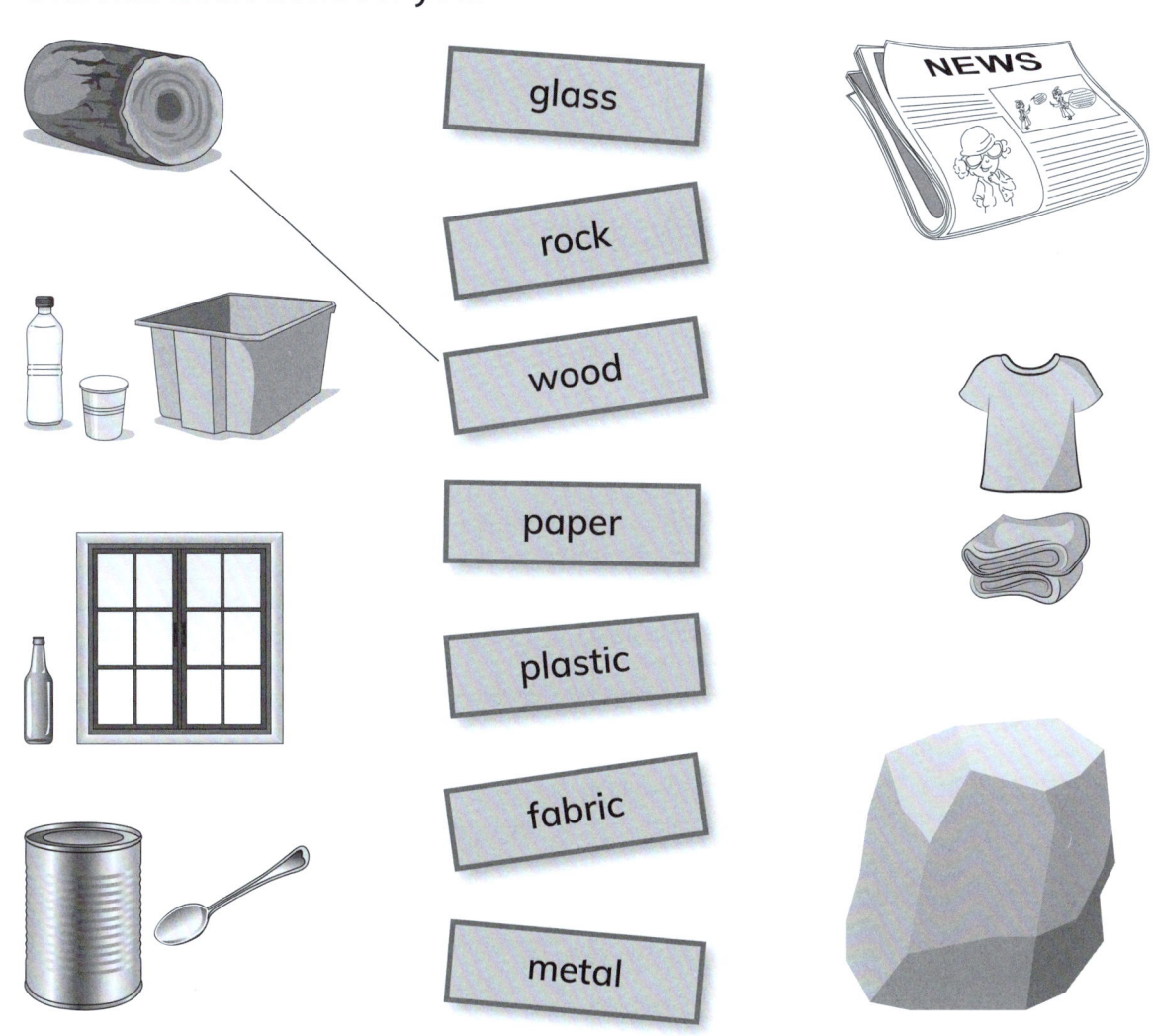

- glass
- rock
- wood
- paper
- plastic
- fabric
- metal

3 Materials in my world

Practice

2. What materials are these things made of?

    Use these words to help you.

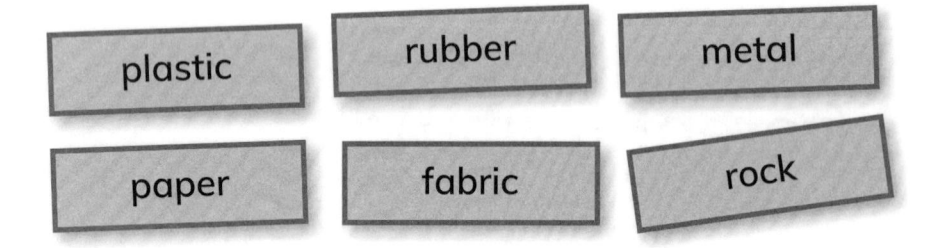

    plastic   rubber   metal
    paper   fabric   rock

    One has been done for you.

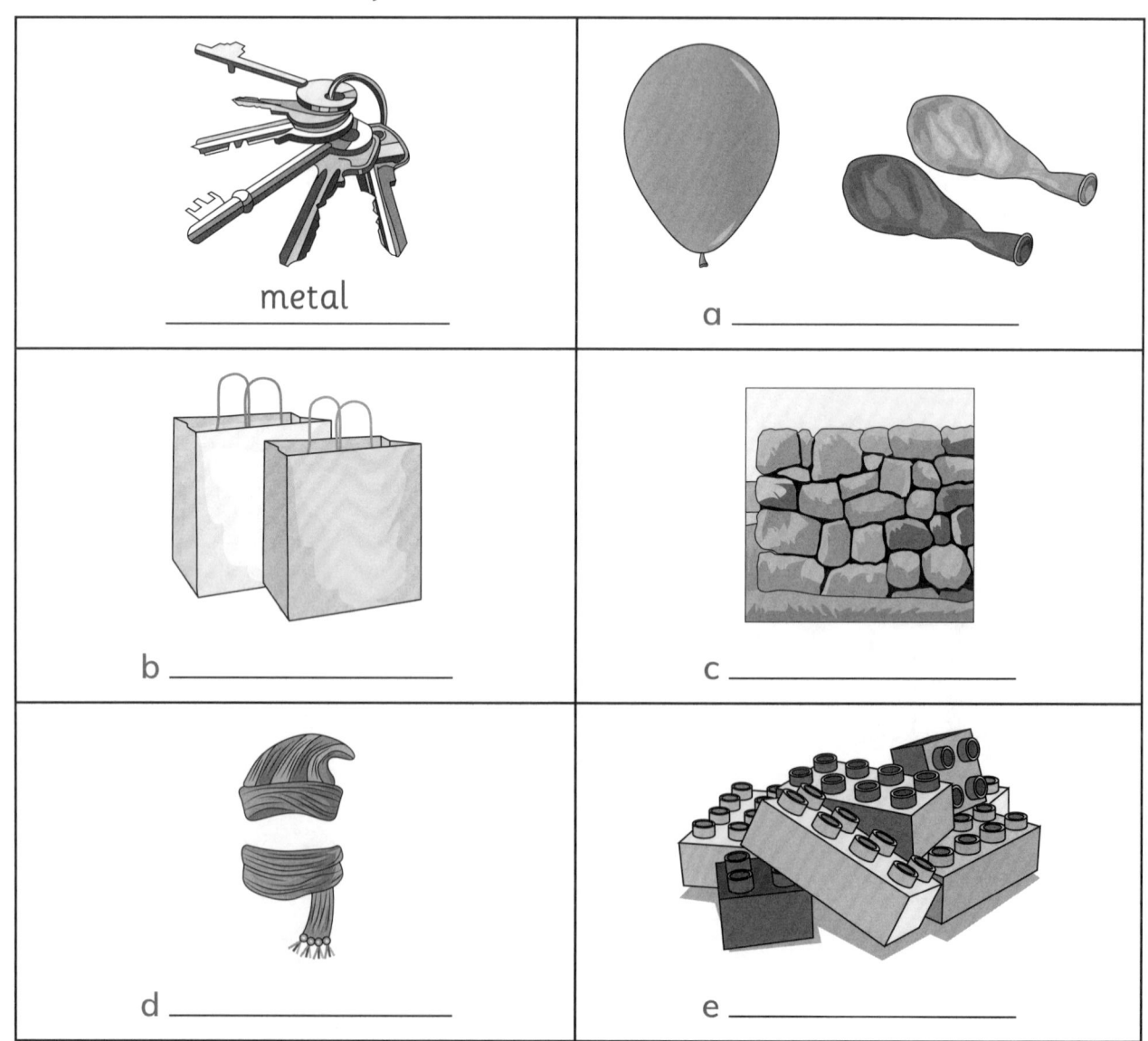

    | metal (keys) | a _____ (balloons) |
    | b _____ (paper bags) | c _____ (stone wall) |
    | d _____ (scarf) | e _____ (lego bricks) |

3.1 Different materials

Challenge

3 What materials are these things made of?

Finish the sentence for each one.

Use words below to help you.

fabric   metal   rock   paper   plastic

a The books are made from _____.

b The clothes are made from _____.

c The water bottles are made from _____.

d The paper clip is made from _____.

e The castle is made from _____.

f The can is made from _____.

25

3 Materials in my world

> 3.2 Properties of materials

Focus

1 Draw a circle around the correct word to describe the object in the picture. The first one has been done for you.

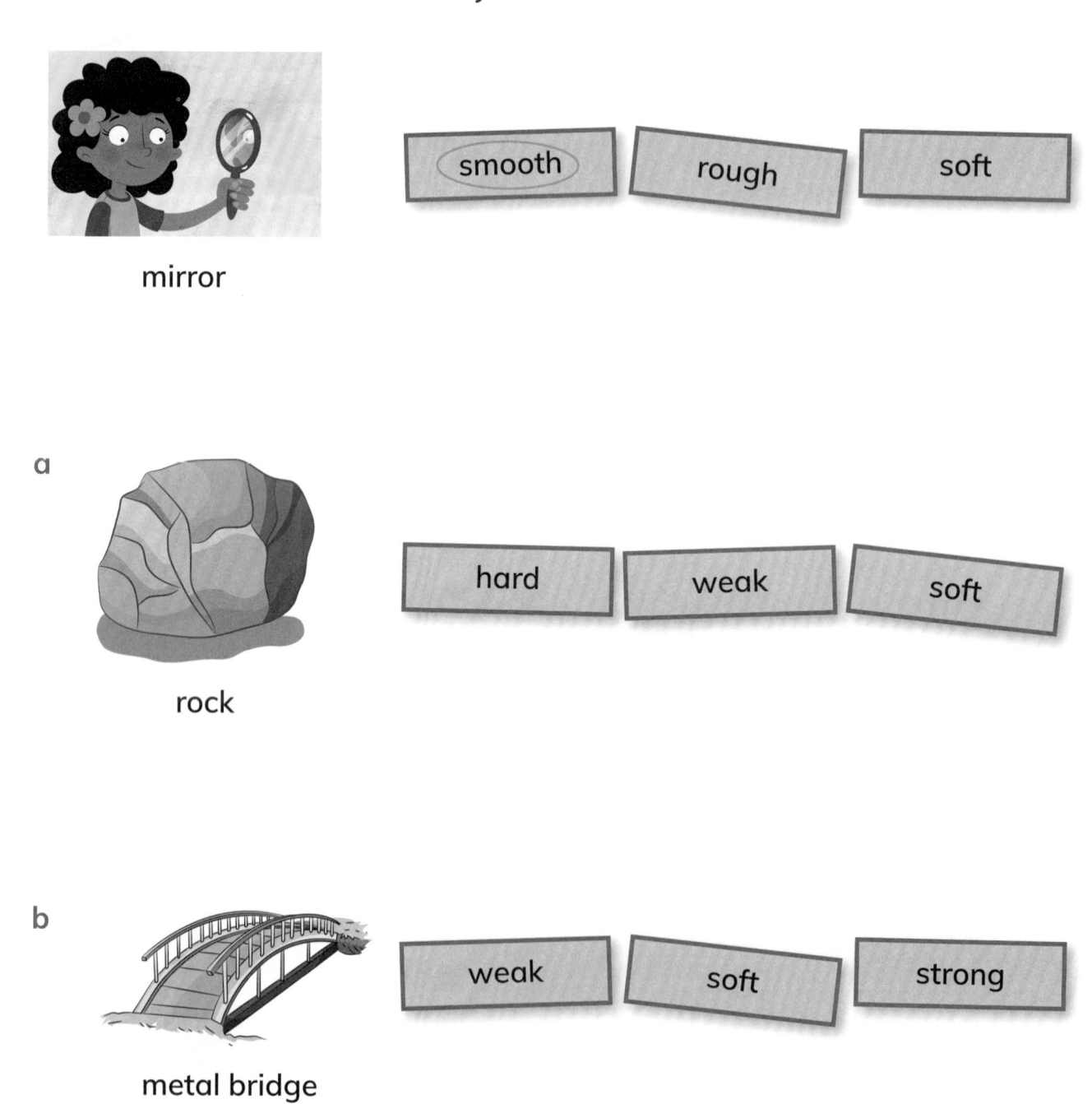

mirror — smooth / rough / soft

a rock — hard / weak / soft

b metal bridge — weak / soft / strong

3.2 Properties of materials

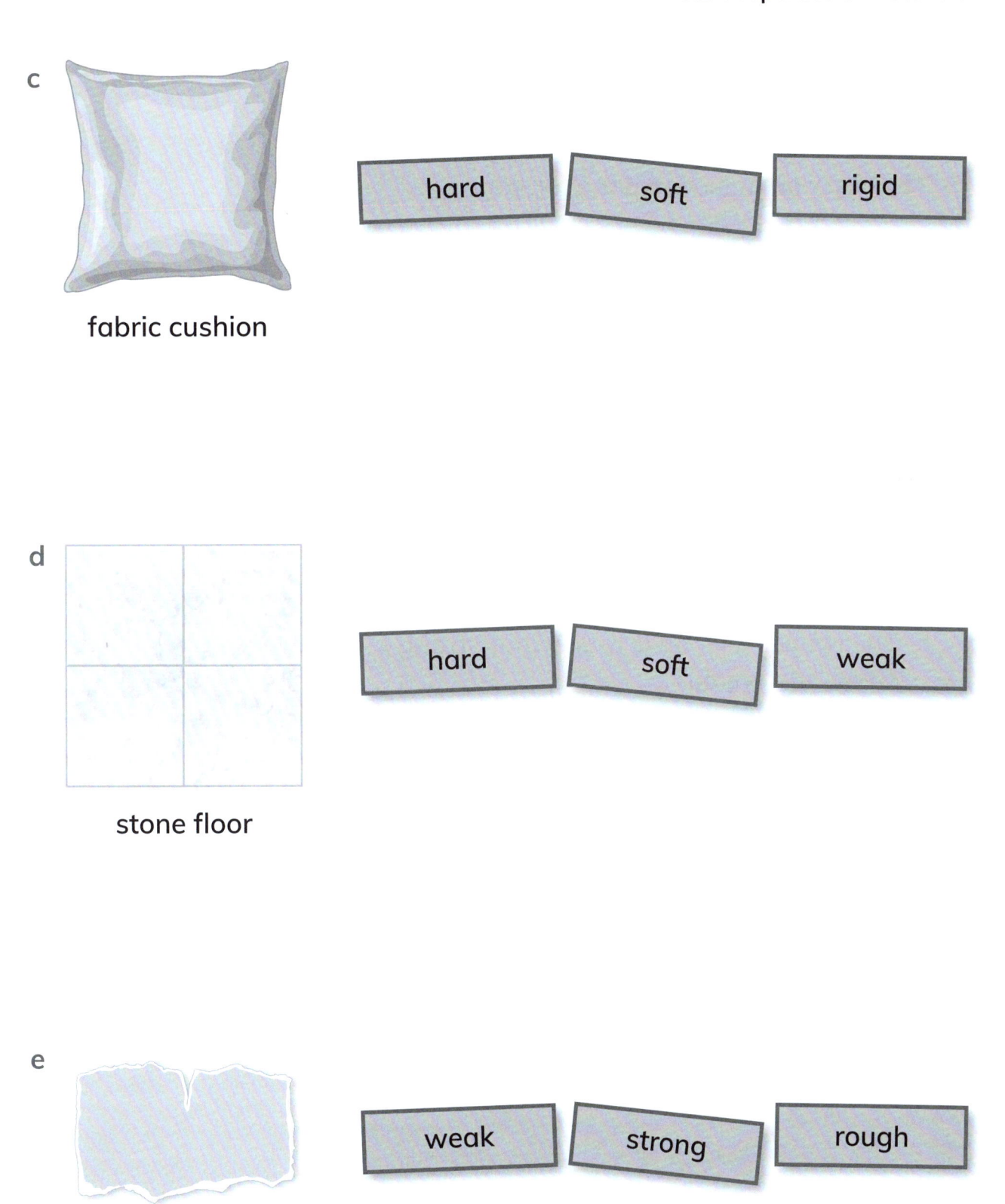

c fabric cushion — hard | soft | rigid

d stone floor — hard | soft | weak

e paper — weak | strong | rough

27

3 Materials in my world

Practice

2 Draw a circle around the right words in these sentences. The first one has been done for you.

The metal can is **weak and soft** / **(strong and shiny)**.

a The brick is **strong and dull** / **weak and soft**.

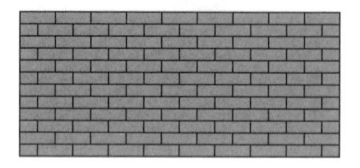

b The rubber balloon is **rough and strong** / **shiny and weak**.

c The rock is **hard and rough** / **soft and smooth**.

d The glass bottle is **soft and rough** / **shiny and smooth**.

e The paper is **rough and strong** / **smooth and weak**.

3.2 Properties of materials

Challenge

3   Choose the right words to finish the sentences.

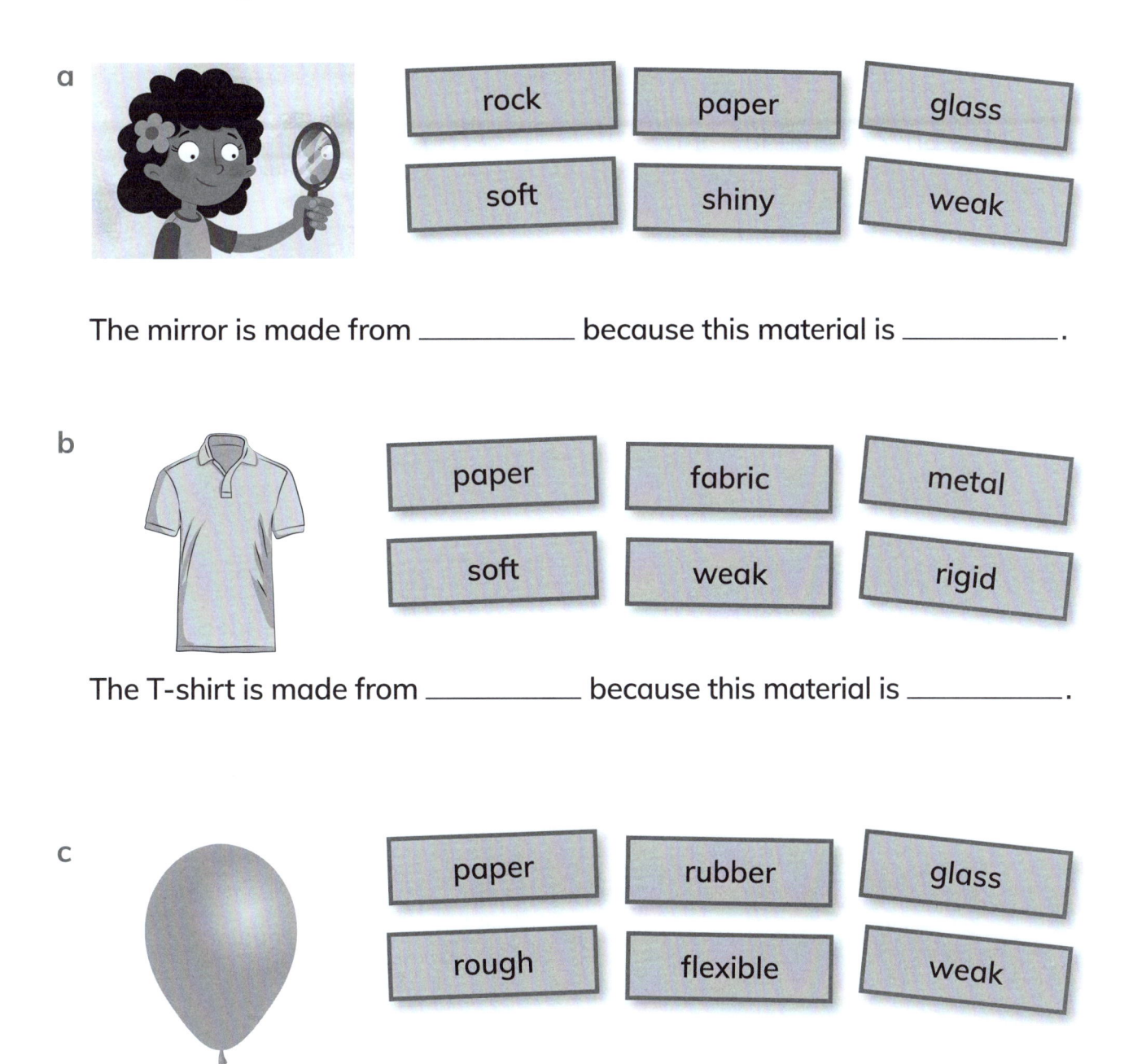

a

| rock | paper | glass |
| soft | shiny | weak |

The mirror is made from _____ because this material is _____.

b

| paper | fabric | metal |
| soft | weak | rigid |

The T-shirt is made from _____ because this material is _____.

c

| paper | rubber | glass |
| rough | flexible | weak |

The balloon is made from _____ because this material is _____.

3 Materials in my world

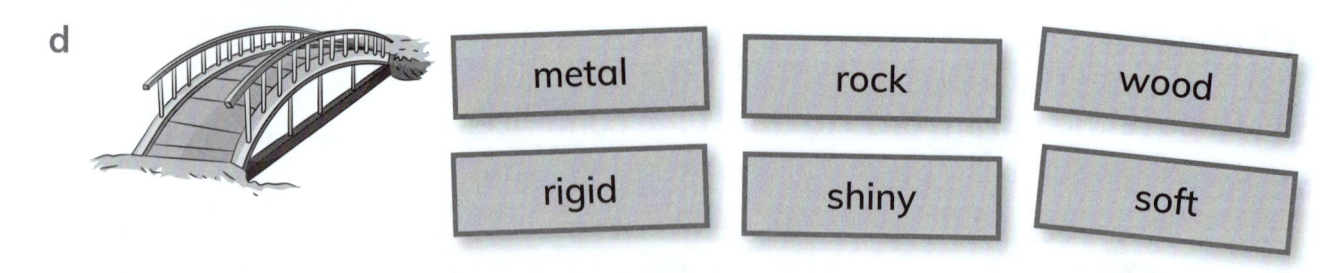

d

| metal | rock | wood |
| rigid | shiny | soft |

The bridge is made from _____ because this material is _____.

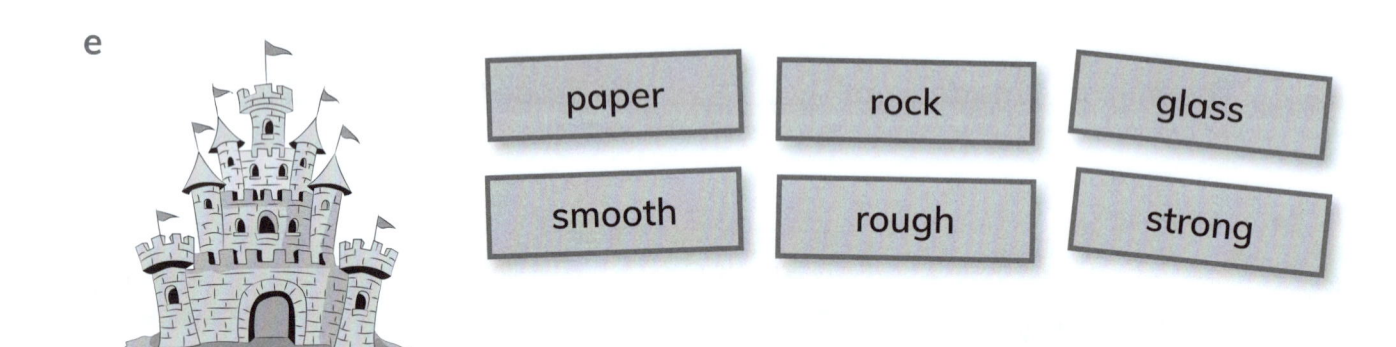

e

| paper | rock | glass |
| smooth | rough | strong |

The castle is made from _____ because this material is _____.

30

> 3.3 Sorting materials

Focus

1 Draw lines from the labels to the correct recycling bins.

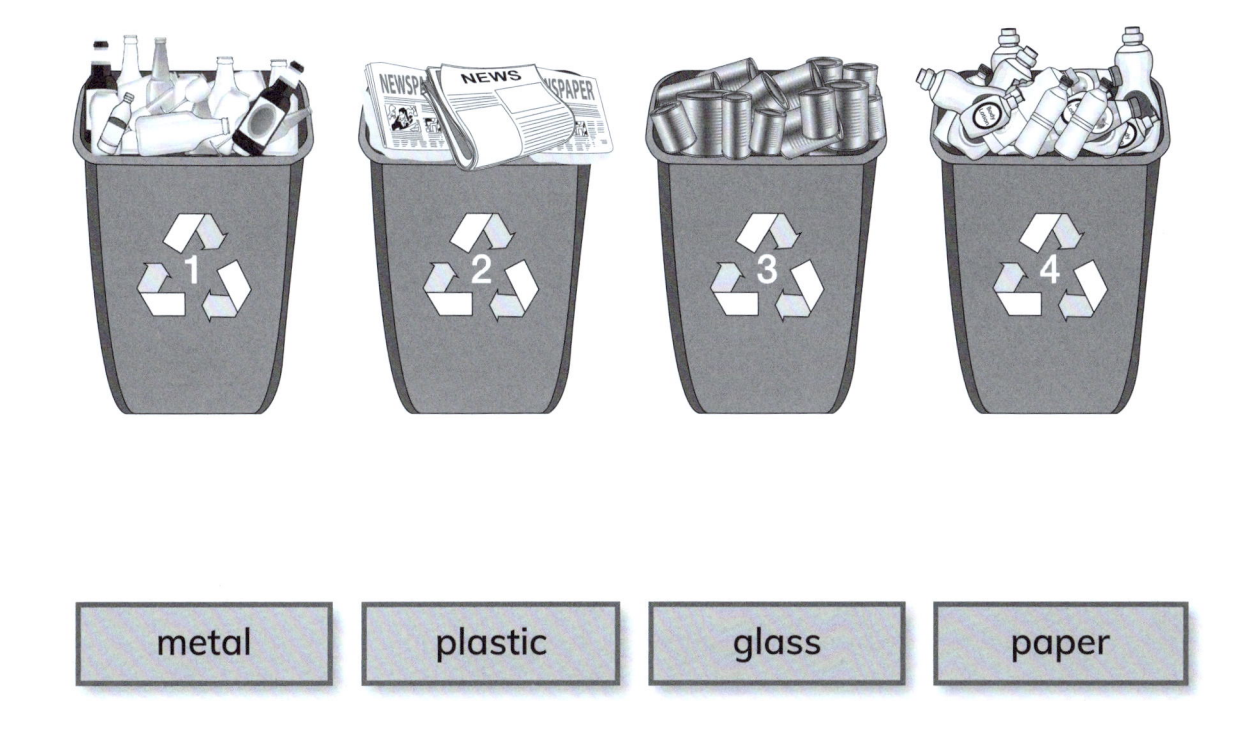

| metal | plastic | glass | paper |

2 Draw a line to show which bin this should go into.

3 Materials in my world

Practice

3 Sort the materials into the right group.

Draw a line from each picture to the correct group.

metal

fabric

hard

plastic

soft

rubber

rock

glass

3.3 Sorting materials

Challenge

4   Draw a circle around the right word to finish these sentences.

   a   Fabric is rigid / hard / flexible.

   b   Metal is rough / strong / weak.

   c   Glass is hard / soft / flexible.

   d   All of these are shiny / fabric / rough.

   e   All of these are hard / flexible / strong.

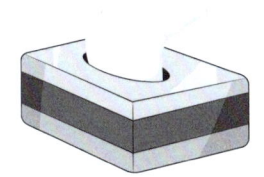

   f   All of these are flexible / rigid / weak.

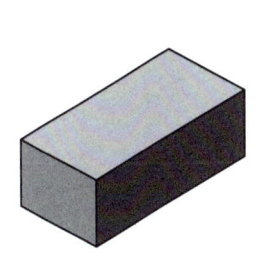

33

3 Materials in my world

> 3.4 Changing materials

Focus

1 Draw a circle around the word that matches each picture.

a

bend / twist / stretch / compress

b

bend / twist / stretch / compress

c

bend / twist / stretch / compress

d

bend / twist / stretch / compress

3.4 Changing materials

Practice

2 Draw a circle around the word that describes what has happened to these materials.

The first one has been done for you.

The can has been bent / twisted / (compressed).

a  The paper has been bent / twisted / compressed.

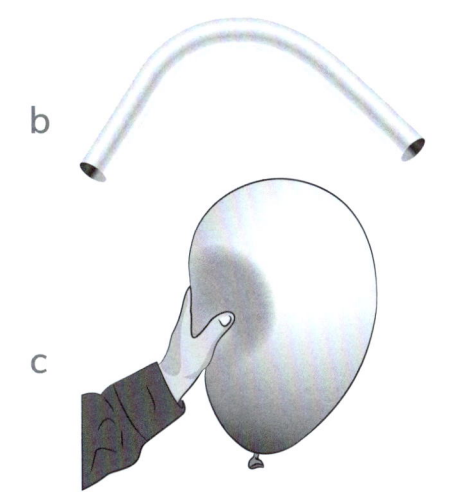

b The pipe has been bent / twisted / compressed.

c The balloon is being bent / twisted / compressed.

d  The rope has been bent / twisted / compressed.

e  The fruit has been bent / twisted / compressed.

3 Materials in my world

Challenge

3 Zara is testing materials.

Finish the table of results.

Material	Compress	Bend
paper	yes	yes
metal		
fabric		
wood		
rubber		
glass		

Use the results to finish these sentences.

Use these words to help you.

| compress | bend |

The first one has been done for you.

Zara can <u>bend</u> the paper.

a Zara cannot _____ the metal.

b Zara can _____ the fabric.

c Zara cannot _____ the wood.

d Zara can _____ the rubber.

e Zara cannot _____ the glass.

4 The Earth

> 4.1 Planet Earth

Focus

1 What does Earth look like from space?

Tick (✓) the sentences that say what an astronaut can see from space.

The Earth is like a ball. ☐	There are clouds on Earth. ☐
There is land on Earth. ☐	There are rivers on Earth. ☐
There are seas on Earth. ☐	There are lakes on Earth. ☐

4 The Earth

Practice

2   Draw a line from the labels to the right place on the Earth.

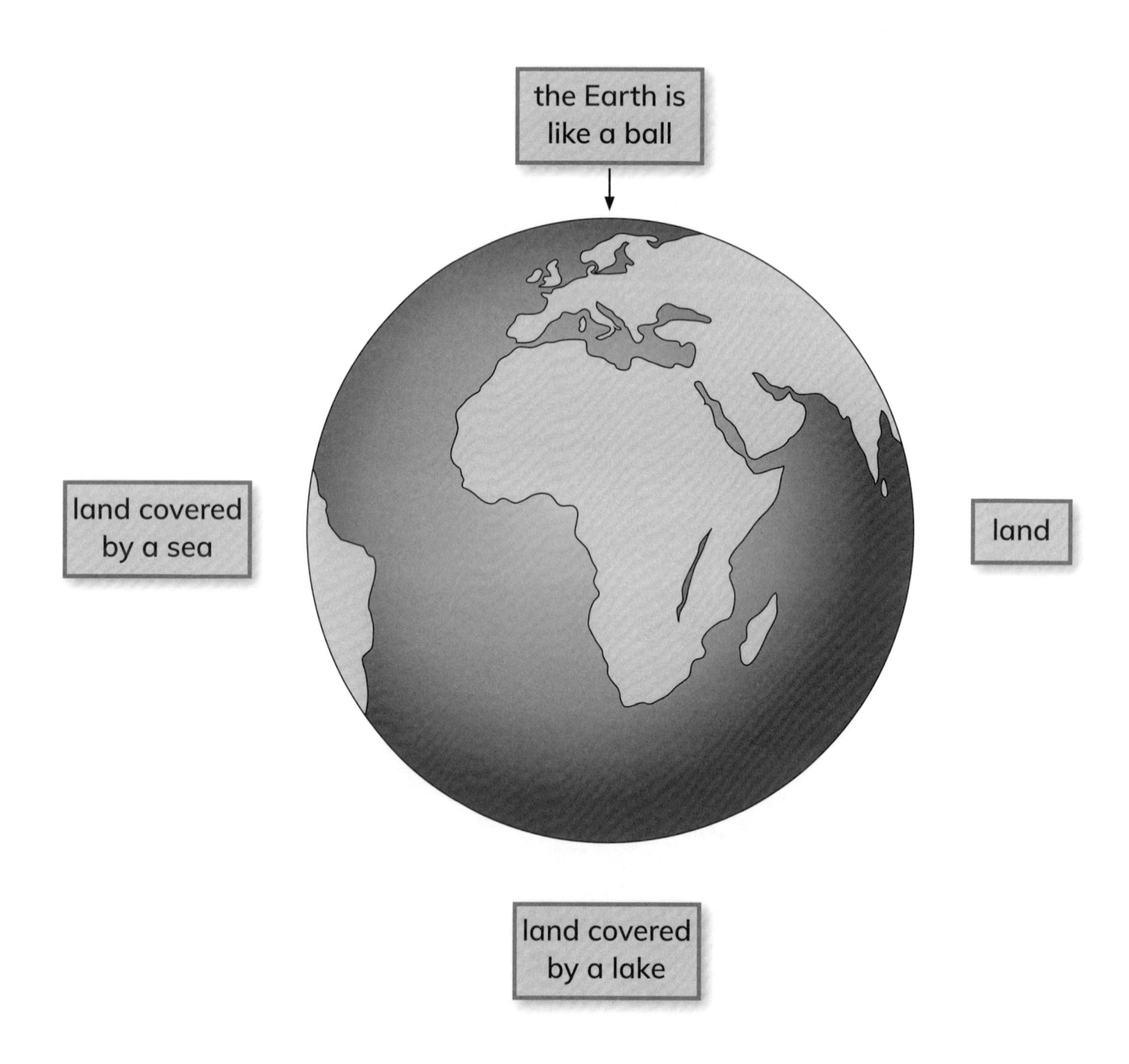

the Earth is like a ball

land covered by a sea

land

land covered by a lake

Challenge

3 Earth is the only planet with life on it.

Write answers to complete the sentences.

Use these words:

| living things | ball | water | land | planet |

a The Earth is like a very large _____.

b The Earth is a _____.

c The surface of the Earth is made of _____.

d Some land is covered with _____.

e Earth is home to lots of _____.

4 The Earth

> 4.2 Heat and light from the Sun

Focus

1 Does light from the Sun help these things?

Draw a circle around the right word, yes or no.

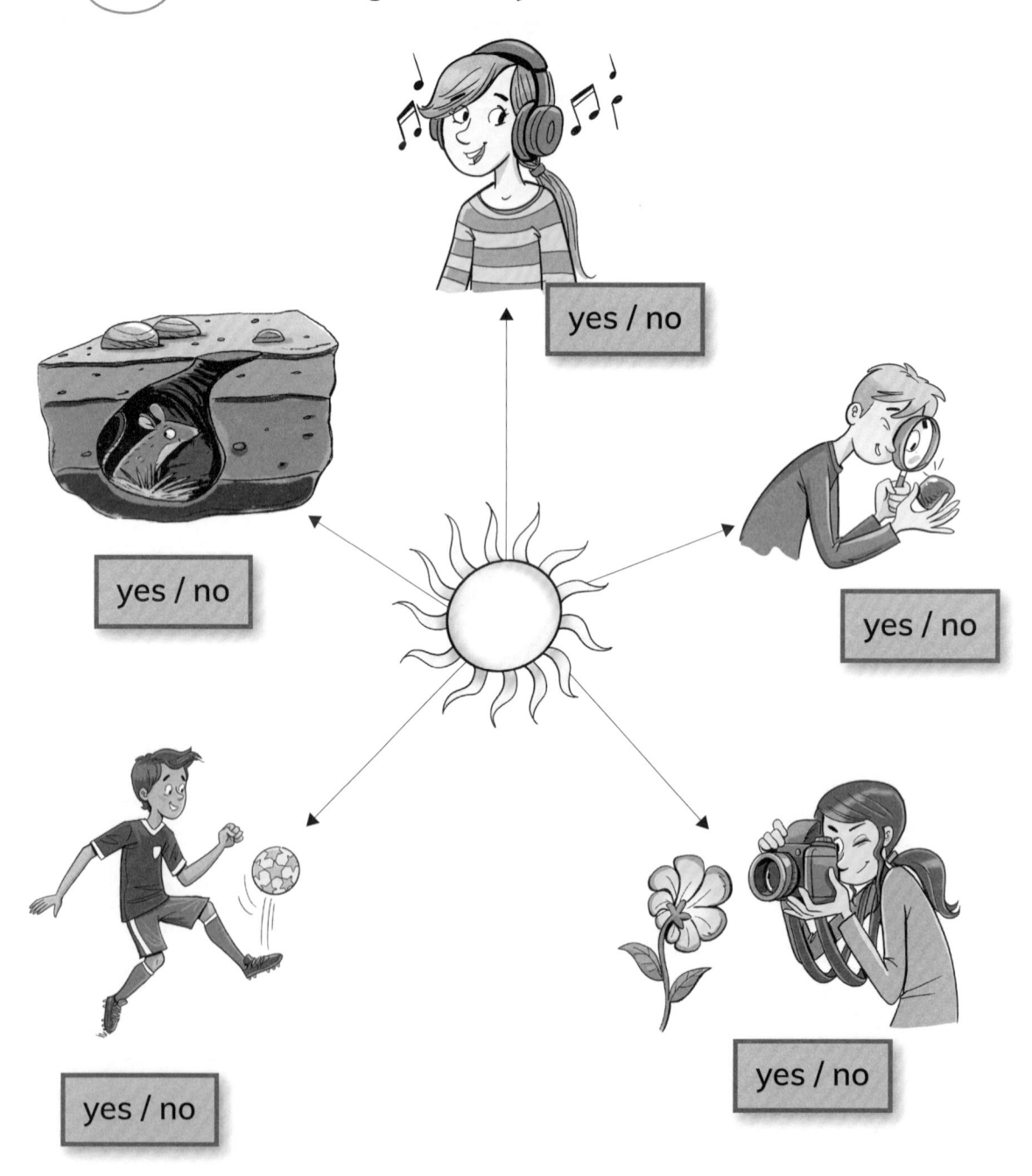

yes / no

yes / no

yes / no

yes / no

yes / no

4.2 Heat and light from the Sun

Practice

2   We get heat and light from the Sun.
    Look at the picture.

41

4 The Earth

Copy the right word to finish each sentence.

a Light from the Sun helps us to _____.

see   warm   cold   hurt   Sun

b Light from the Sun can _____.

see   warm   cold   hurt our eyes

c At night there is no light from the _____.

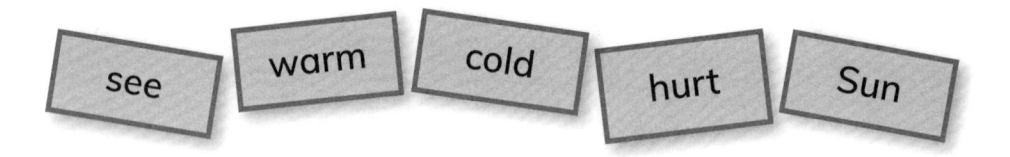

see   warm   cold   hurt   Sun

d The Sun gives us heat to keep us _____.

see   warm   cold   hurt   Sun

e Without heat from the Sun we would be very _____.

see   warm   cold   hurt   Sun

4.2 Heat and light from the Sun

Challenge

3   On planet Earth the light from the Sun gives us daytime.

After our daytime we get night-time.

Zara and Marcus have a model of day and night on planet Earth.

The flashlight is the Sun.

Use these words to label the model.

| day | Earth | night |

4   Marcus, holding the flashlight, can only see one side of Earth.

Draw a circle around the right word in this sentence.

He can see the **day side / night side** of the Earth.

4 The Earth

> 4.3 Rocks

Focus

1 Look at the two different rocks.
   Write the name of each rock below the pictures.

   _____   _____

2 How are the rocks different?

   Which rock is harder? _____

   Which rock is smoother? _____

3 How are the rocks the same? Draw a (circle) around the right answers.

   Both rocks are strong.   Both rocks are weak.

   Both rocks are flexible.   Both rocks are rigid.

4.3 Rocks

Practice

4 Sofia tries to scratch these rocks with a metal nail.
   She wants to name the rocks.

> **Granite** – very hard with different coloured bits
>
> **Chalk** – soft, white
>
> **Limestone** – hard, grey

Draw a ⓒircle around the correct name for each rock.

Rock A is **chalk / limestone / granite.**

Rock B is **chalk / limestone / granite.**

Rock C is **chalk / limestone / granite.**

4 The Earth

Challenge

5 Marcus uses a wooden stick to scratch rocks.

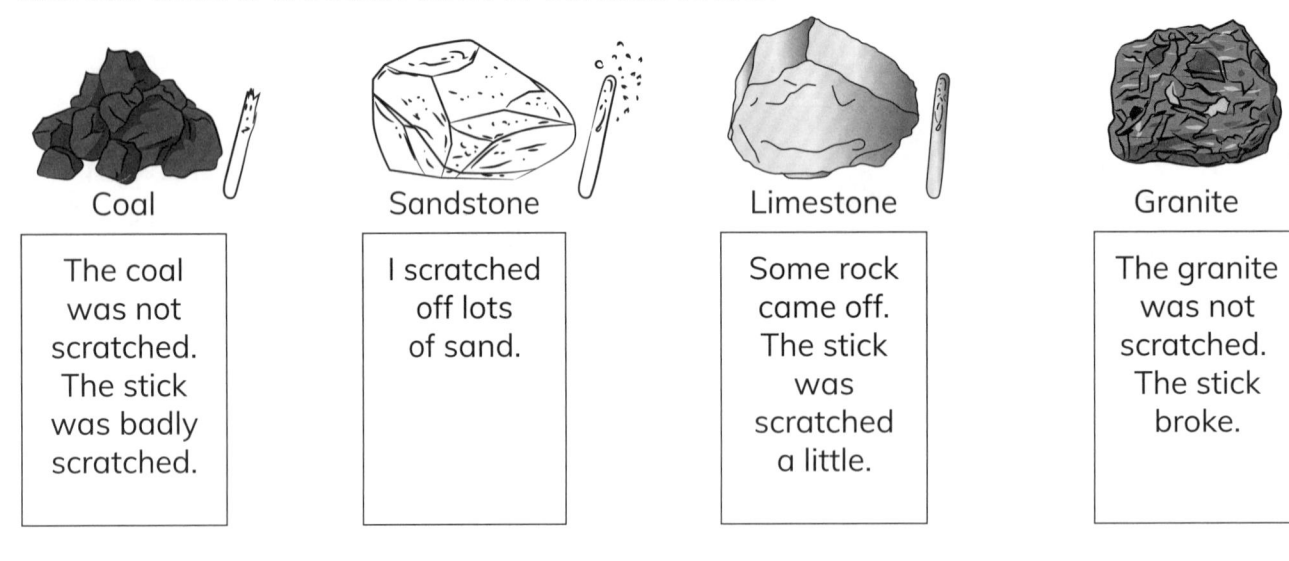

Coal	Sandstone	Limestone	Granite
The coal was not scratched. The stick was badly scratched.	I scratched off lots of sand.	Some rock came off. The stick was scratched a little.	The granite was not scratched. The stick broke.

Copy the right word to finish each sentence.

a The hardest rock was _____.

hard   sandstone   granite   soft

b The softest rock was _____.

hard   sandstone   granite   soft

c The granite broke the stick because it is _____.

hard   sandstone   granite   soft

d Sandstone did not damage the stick because it is _____.

hard   sandstone   granite   soft

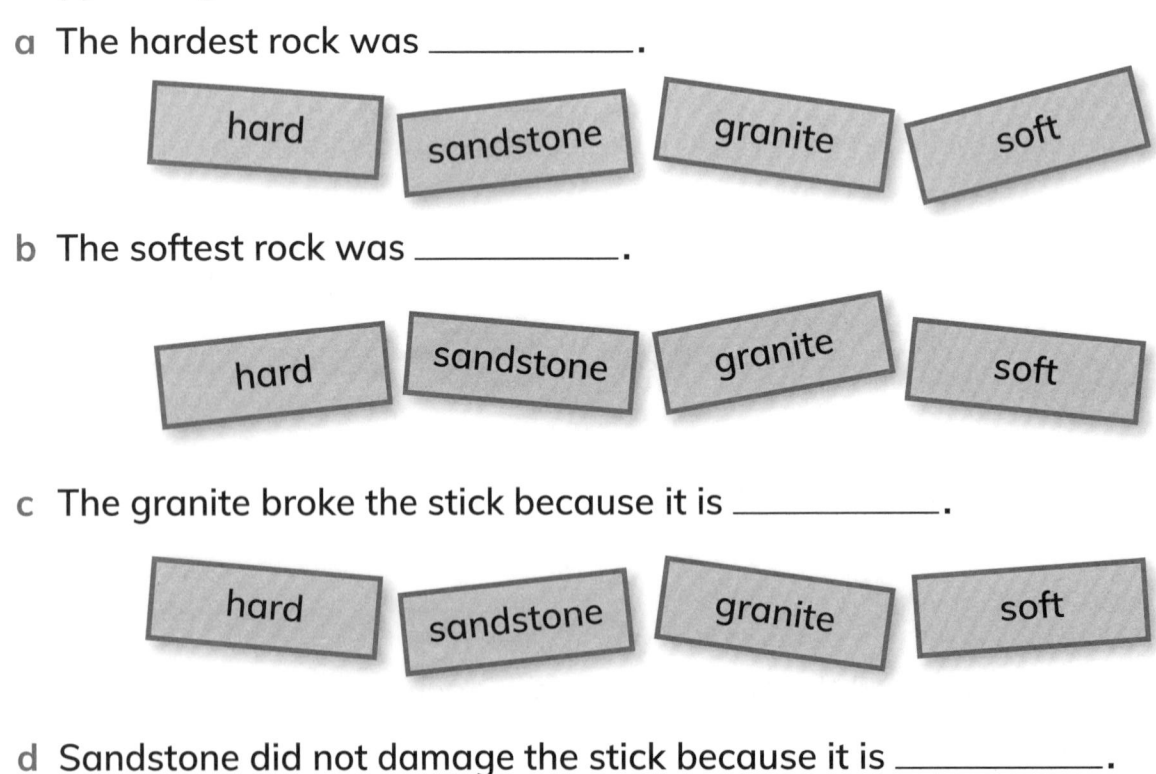

> 4.4 Soil

Focus

1 Look at the picture of the carrot growing in soil.

  Read what the children said.

  Cross out (~~cross out~~) the things that are wrong.
  Tick the things that are right.
  One has been done for you.

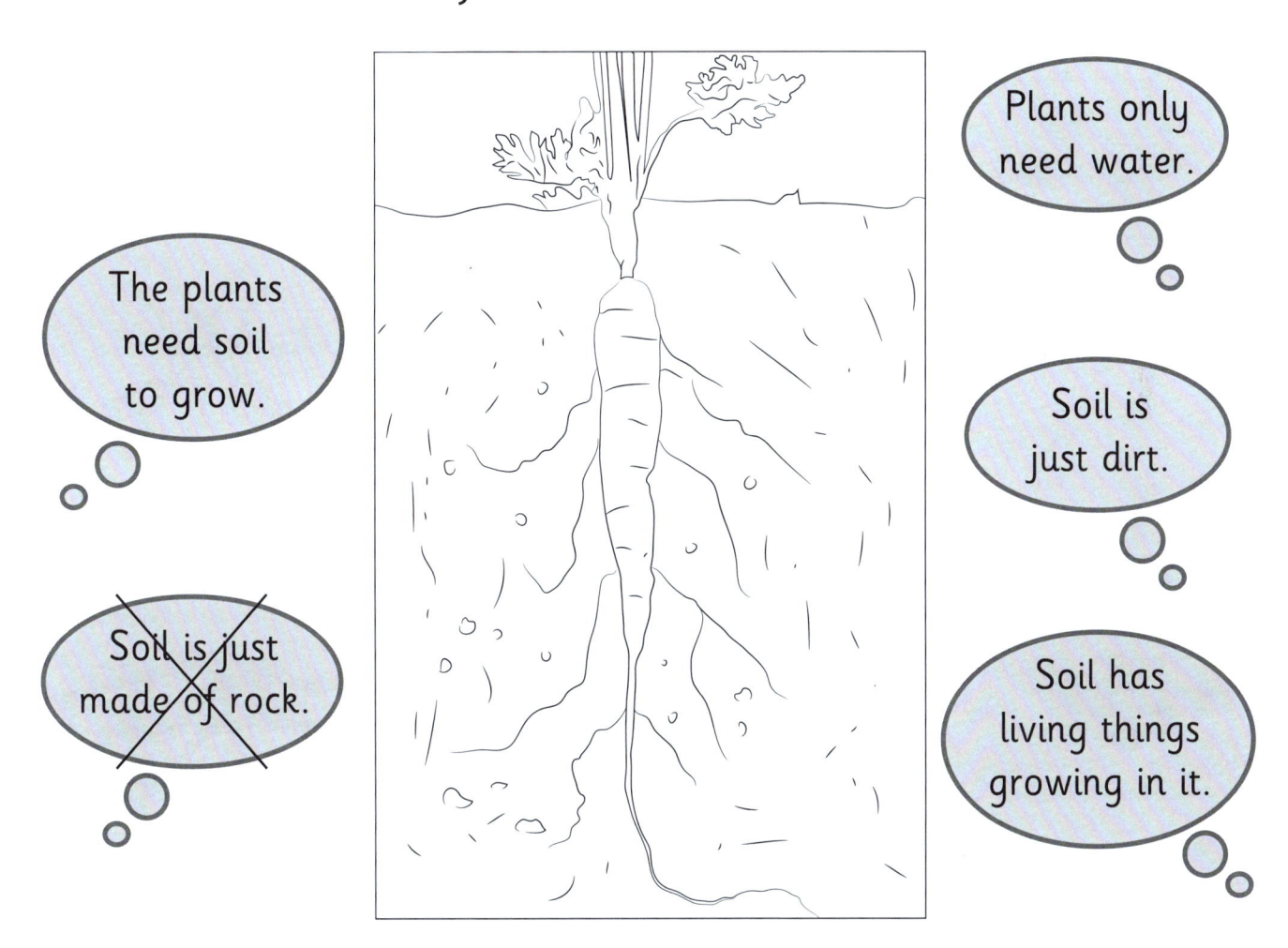

  - The plants need soil to grow.
  - ~~Soil is just made of rock.~~
  - Plants only need water.
  - Soil is just dirt.
  - Soil has living things growing in it.

4 The Earth

Practice

2 Look at the eight things around the hands holding the plant. Draw a (circle) around the ones which you find in the soil.

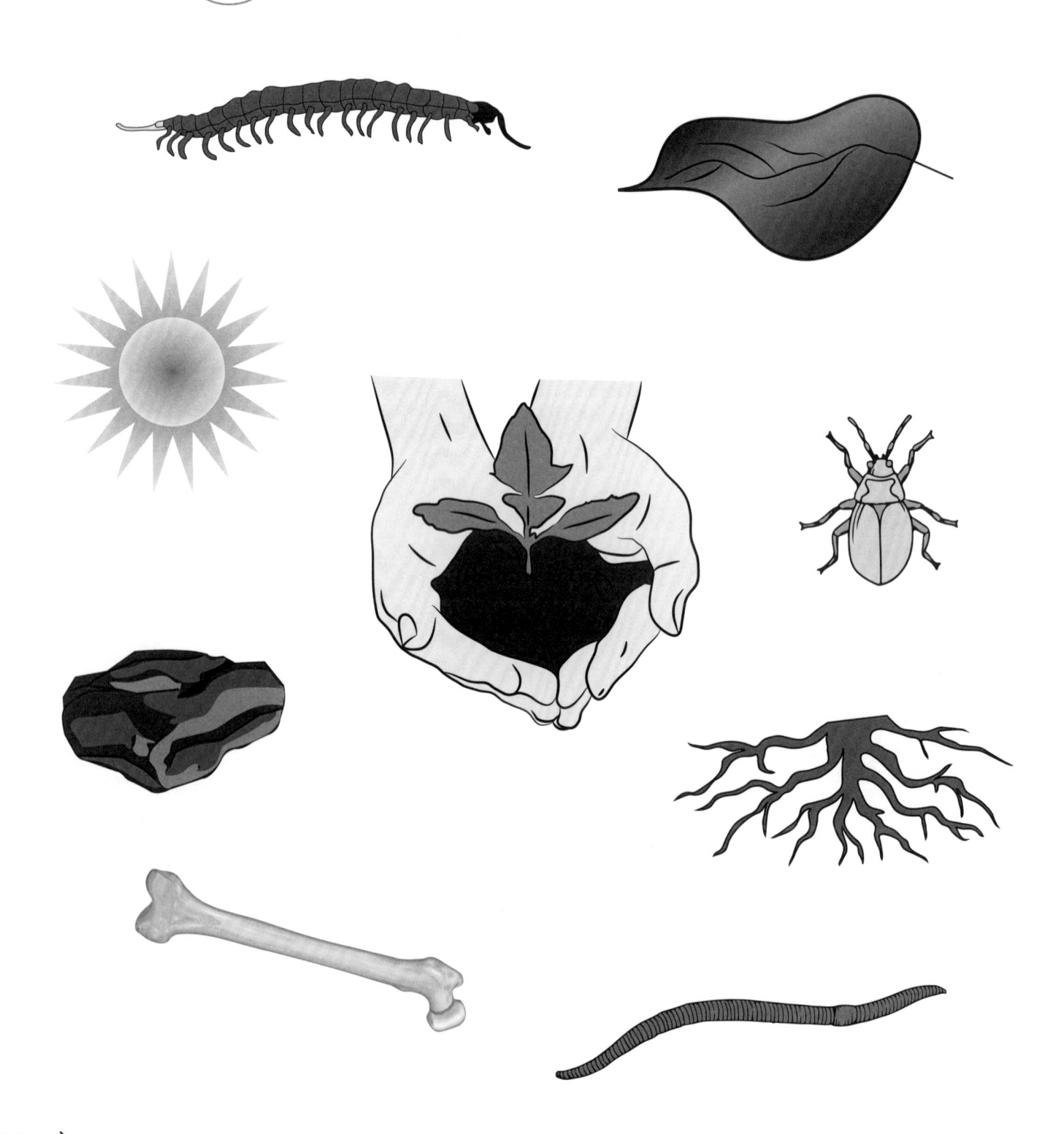

4.4 Soil

Challenge

3 Arun and Marcus are looking at two different soils.

One soil is from the park and the other soil is from the school garden.

They record the things they found.

In soil from the park we found...	In soil from the school garden we found...
rocks	beetle
	dead leaf
	bone
	earthworm
	rocks

Which is the better soil?

Draw a circle around the correct word in this sentence.

The soil from the park / garden is better.

Why is this a better soil?

It is better because it has _____

_____

49

5 Humans

> 5.1 Our bodies

Focus

1 Draw lines from the words in boxes to label the drawing of the body.

- eye
- nose
- hair
- mouth
- shoulder
- ear
- chest
- elbow
- hip
- hand
- knee
- finger
- foot
- tummy
- toe

5.1 Our bodies

Practice

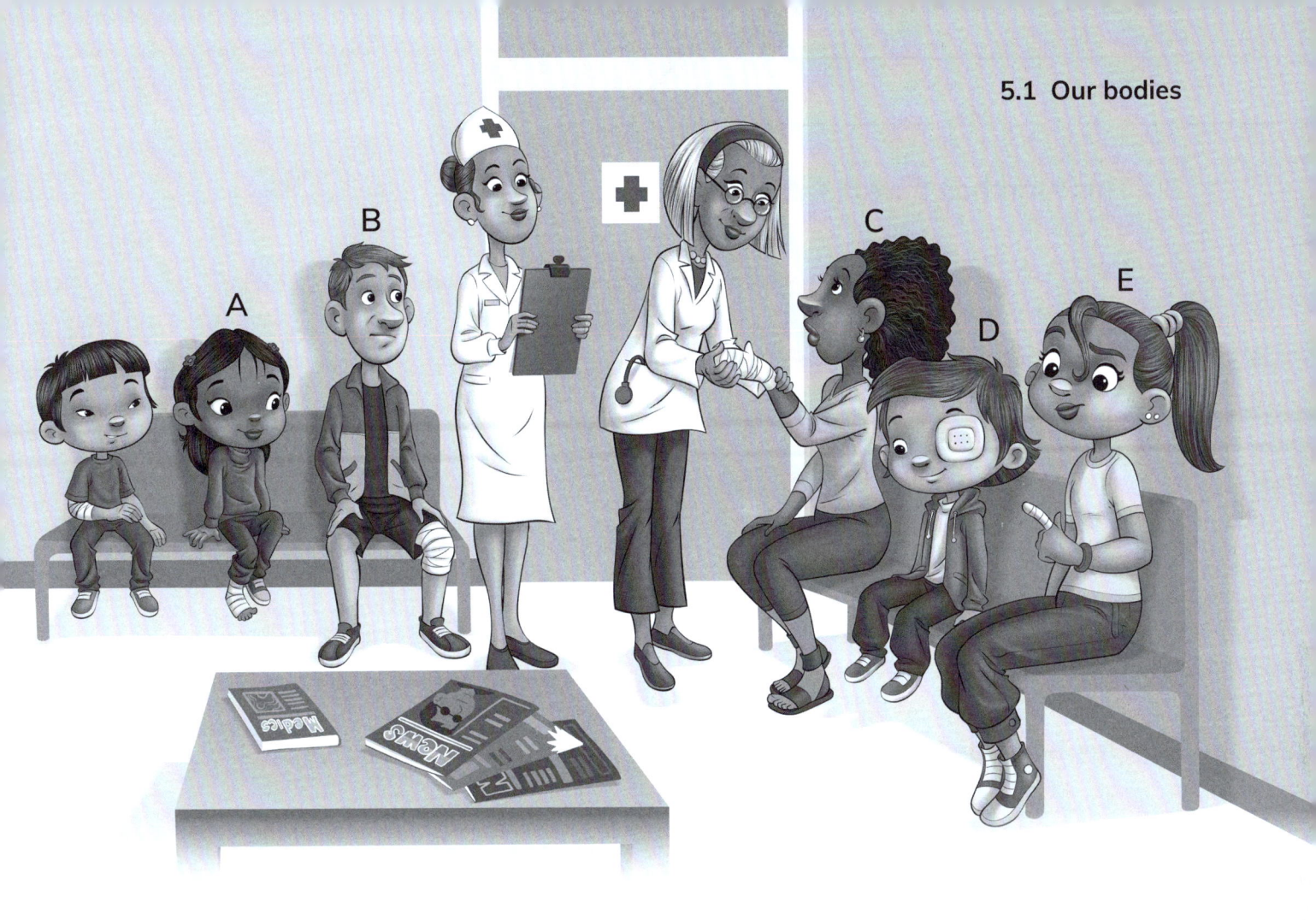

2 These people are hurt.
   Draw a circle around the correct word to finish these sentences.
   The first one has been done for you.

   The boy next to girl A has hurt his _____.

   foot   (elbow)   knee

A This girl has hurt her _____.

   knee   foot   finger

5 Humans

B   This man has hurt his _____.

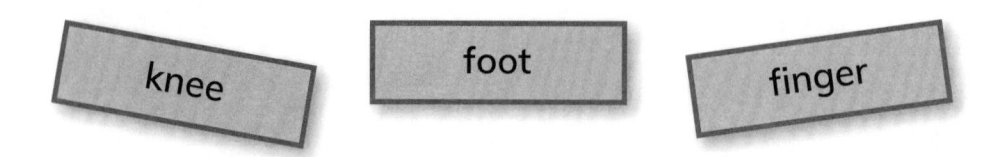

> knee   foot   finger

C   This woman has hurt her _____.

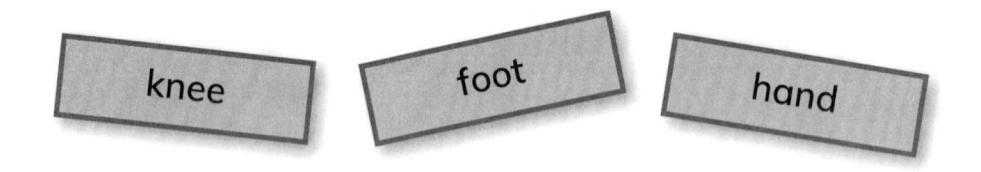

> knee   foot   hand

D   This boy has hurt his _____.

> finger   hand   eye

E   This girl has hurt her _____.

> finger   hand   eye

5.1 Our bodies

Challenge

3 These children are comparing their feet.

Amna	Bill	Arun	Fen
Example: 8 bricks	__ bricks	__ bricks	__ bricks

Fill in the gaps in the table to show how many bricks for Bill, Arun and Fen.

Who has the longest feet?

Draw a circle around the correct answer.

| Amna | Bill | Arun | Fen |

Who has the shortest feet?

Draw a circle around the correct answer.

| Amna | Bill | Arun | Fen |

5 Humans

> 5.2 Our amazing senses

Focus

1 Colour in red the things you can smell.

   Colour in blue the things you can hear.

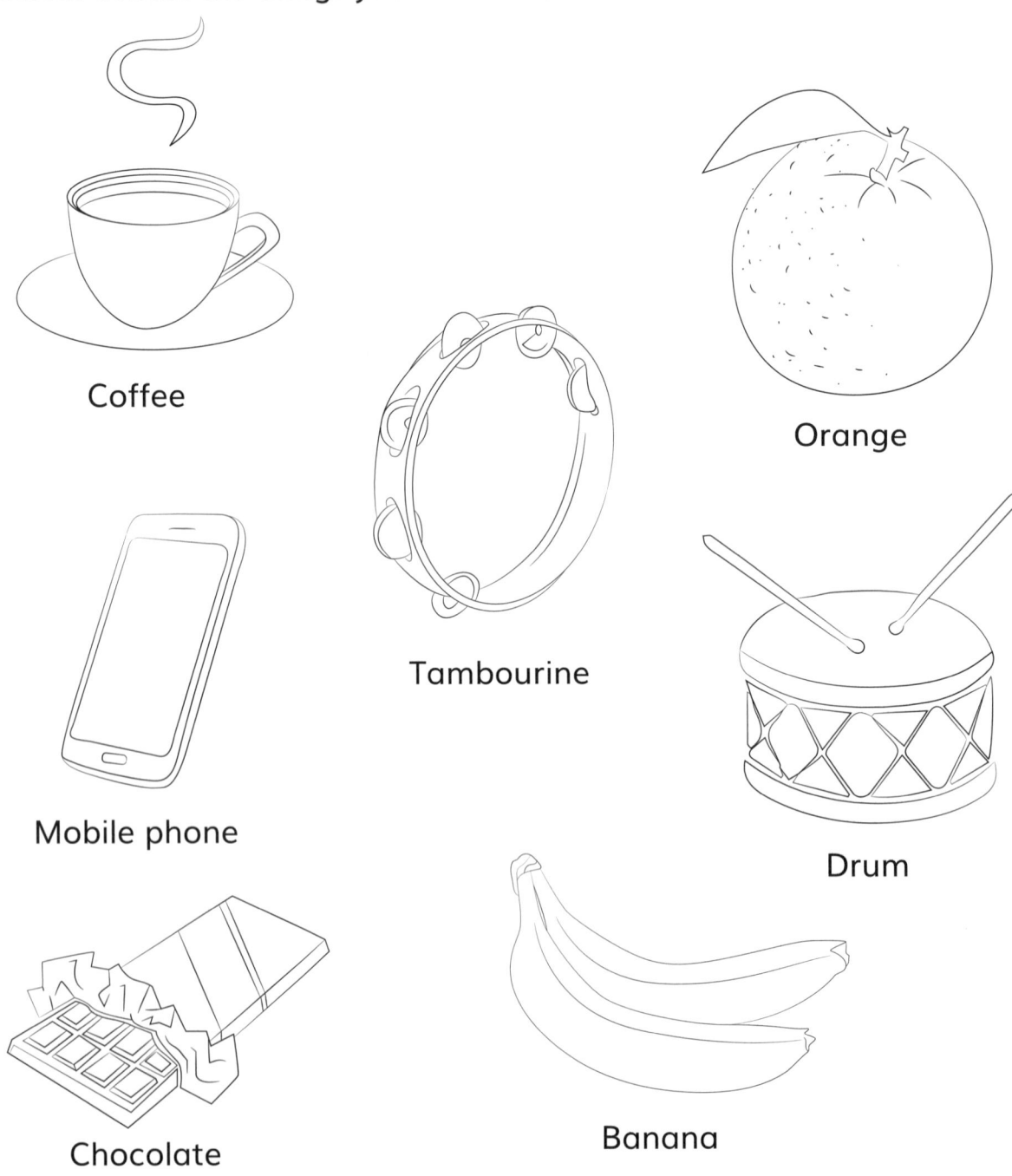

Coffee

Orange

Tambourine

Mobile phone

Drum

Chocolate

Banana

5.2 Our amazing senses

Practice

2 Draw lines to match the senses to the right place on the picture.

hearing

taste

sight

smell

touch

55

5 Humans

3 Copy the right word to finish each sentence. The first one has been done for you.

You touch with your ____skin____.

skin   eyes   nose   ears   mouth

a You hear with your _____.

skin   eyes   nose   ears   mouth

b You see with your _____.

skin   eyes   nose   ears   mouth

c You taste with your _____.

skin   eyes   nose   ears   mouth

d You smell with your _____.

skin   eyes   nose   ears   mouth

5.2 Our amazing senses

Challenge

4   Alex is investigating touch.

His predictions for what he touched and his results are in this table.

	A	B	C
Prediction	orange	book	pencil
Result	lemon	book	pen

| Was he right? | Yes / (No) | Yes / No | Yes / No |

Draw a (circle) around the missing answers for columns B and C.

How many predictions were right? _____

How many predictions were wrong? _____

5 Humans

> 5.3 Similar and different

Focus

1 Draw a friend in each box, then write their name in the box and on the right line.

Taller than me

_____

Shorter than me

_____

Same colour hair as me

_____

Different colour hair to me

_____

5.3 Similar and different

Practice

2   Look at these children.

Are these sentences right?

Tick (✓) the right box.

The first one has been done for you.

	They both have arms.	Yes ✔	No ☐
a	They have different skin colour.	Yes ☐	No ☐
b	They are a different height.	Yes ☐	No ☐
c	They have similar hair.	Yes ☐	No ☐
d	They both have eyes.	Yes ☐	No ☐
e	They are both boys.	Yes ☐	No ☐

5 Humans

Challenge

3   Put these people into groups. Write their names in the correct box.

Some of the people will be in more than one group!

short	tall

black hair	fair hair

> 5.4 Staying alive

Focus

1 Udom and Kanya are on holiday.

Colour in only the things they need to stay alive.

5 Humans

Practice

2 Which of these foods are healthy for humans?

Tick (✓) the right box.

The first one has been done for you.

Fruit

Healthy ✔   Not healthy ☐

a Vegetables

Healthy ☐   Not healthy ☐

b Cake

Healthy ☐   Not healthy ☐

c Eggs

Healthy ☐   Not healthy ☐

d Noodles

Healthy ☐   Not healthy ☐

e Sweets

Healthy ☐   Not healthy ☐

5.4 Staying alive

Challenge

3 Finish these sentences.

Use these words.

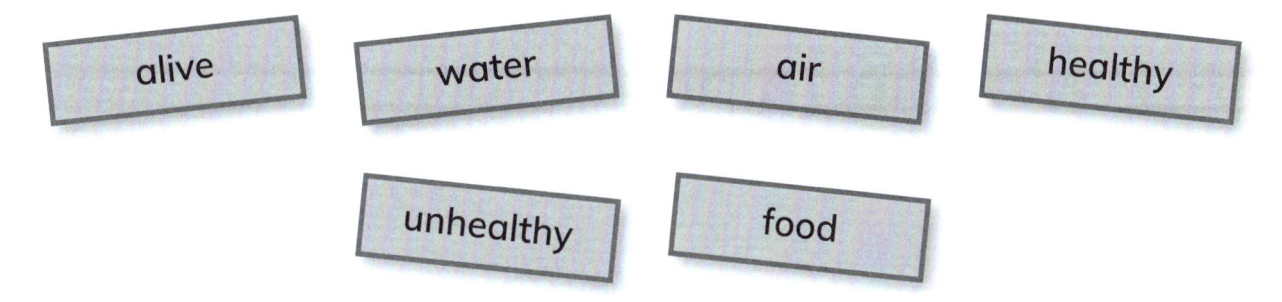

| alive | water | air | healthy |

| unhealthy | food |

a All animals need _____.

b All animals need _____.

c All animals need _____.

d Humans need these things to stay _____.

e If you eat the wrong food you will be _____.

6 Forces

> 6.1 Moving things

Focus

1. The picture shows a playground.

   Some people are moving.

   Some people are not moving.

   How are some people moving?

   Colour in only the people who are moving.

6.1 Moving things

Practice

2   Things move all around us.

Some things have lots of moving parts.

A bicycle has lots of moving parts.

Look at this picture of Zara riding her bicycle.

Draw a circle around the moving parts of the bicycle.

6 Forces

Challenge

3 These toys all move.

Draw a (circle) around one or more of the arrows to show how each one moves.

The first one has been done for you.

| Key | ⤴ rocking | ⟳ rotating | → moving forwards or backwards |

> 6.2 Push and pull forces

Focus

1 We can push or pull lots of things.

   Draw a circle around the correct word or words for each picture.

push / pull   push / pull   push / pull

push / pull   push / pull

push / pull   push / pull

push / pull   push / pull

6 Forces

Practice

2 Think about all the things you move when at home and at school.

Think of things you have pushed and things you have pulled.

Draw pictures of three things that move when you push them.

Draw pictures of three things that move when you pull them.

6.2 Push and pull forces

Challenge

3 This is an arrow: ⟶

Draw arrows on the pictures to show pushes.

a Show the push that the boy gives to the ball.

b Show the push that the girl gives to the ball.

6 Forces

4 Use the pictures to help you to complete the sentences.
Copy the right word to finish each sentence.

a The boy pushes the ball with his _____.

harder   head   little   foot

b The girl pushes the ball with her _____.

harder   head   little   foot

c They can make the ball go faster by pushing it _____.

harder   head   little   foot

d They can make it go slowly with a _____.

harder   head   little push   foot

Think about how you push next time you play with a ball.

> 6.3 Making things move

Focus

1 Some things need a little push or pull force.

   Some things need a big push or pull force.

   Draw a circle around the biggest push.

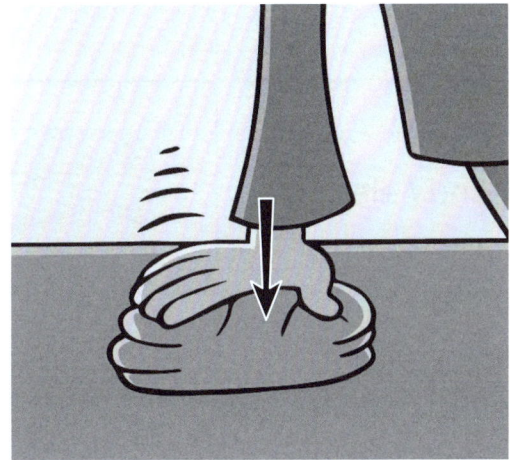

   Draw a circle around the biggest pull.

6 Forces

Practice

2 All these things move.

Some are pushed by hand. Some are moved by electricity.

Draw a circle around the right word for each picture in the table.

(wagon)	hand / electric	(hair dryer)	hand / electric
(toy train)	hand / electric	(toy car)	hand / electric
(fan)	hand / electric	(bucket and spade)	hand / electric
(toy plane)	hand / electric	(hand mixer)	hand / electric
(ceiling fan)	hand / electric	(doll)	hand / electric
(soccer ball)	hand / electric	(skipping rope)	hand / electric

6.3 Making things move

Challenge

3 Sofia gives a big push and the ball goes a long way.

It goes a long way.

Look at the table below.

With a big push, will the car or ball go a long way or a short way?

With a small push, will the car or ball go a long way or a short way?

In the table draw a circle around 'a long way' or 'a short way'.

🚗 (big)	🚗 (small)	⚽ (big)	⚽ (small)
➡️ (big)	➡ (small)	➡️ (big)	➡ (small)
a long way	a long way	a long way	a long way
a short way	a short way	a short way	a short way

73

6 Forces

> 6.4 Floating and sinking

Focus

1   Some things float.

Some things sink.

Make a prediction about each of the things below. Will they float or sink?

Draw each thing in the right box to show your prediction.

Will it float or sink?

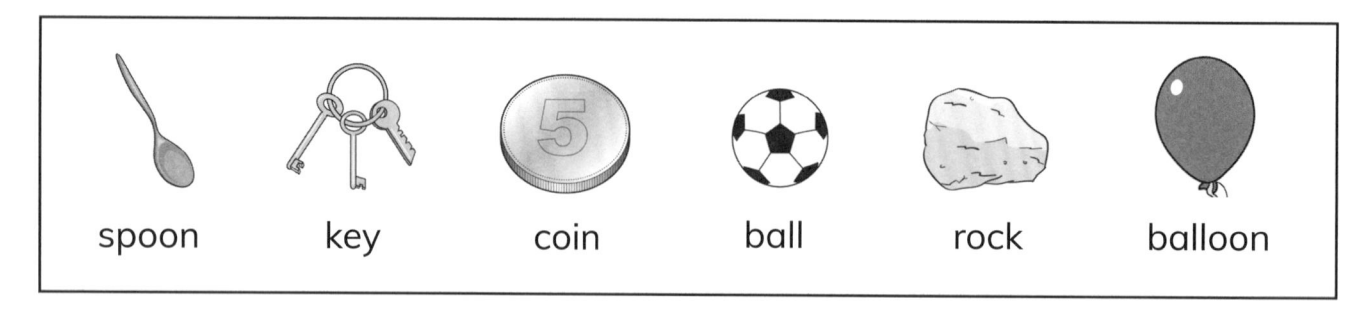

| spoon | key | coin | ball | rock | balloon |

I predict these will float

I predict these will sink

6.4 Floating and sinking

Practice

2 You can change the shape of some things that don't float.

You can change them so that they float.

Look at these clay shapes.

Draw a (circle) around the shapes that will float.

Put a cross (✗) on the shapes that will sink.

Draw another shape that will sink.

Draw another shape that will float.

6 Forces

Challenge

3 Look at the picture.

The metal spoon sinks.

The beach ball floats high in the water.

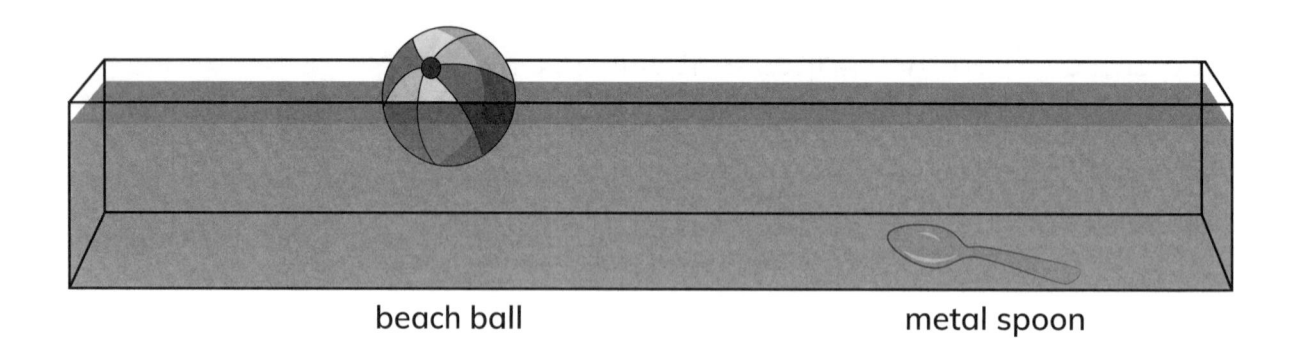

beach ball   metal spoon

Now look at these things.

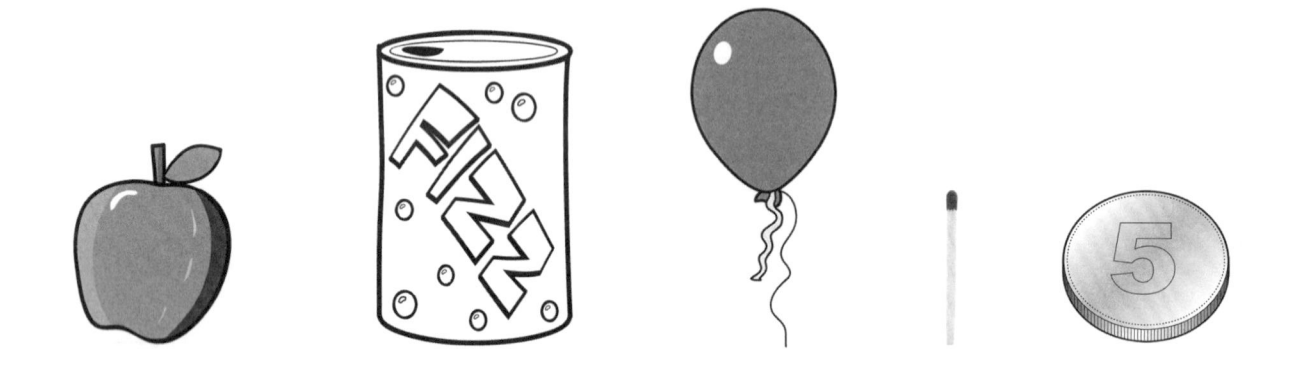

Some things float high in the water.

Some float lower or sink.

a Predict which will float high and which will float lower.

b Draw these things in the tray of water floating high or low.

c Draw the thing that sinks in the tray of water.

> 6.5 Magnets can pull

Focus

1. Some materials are magnetic.

   Many materials are not magnetic.

   Group the magnetic materials together.

   Group the non-magnetic materials together.

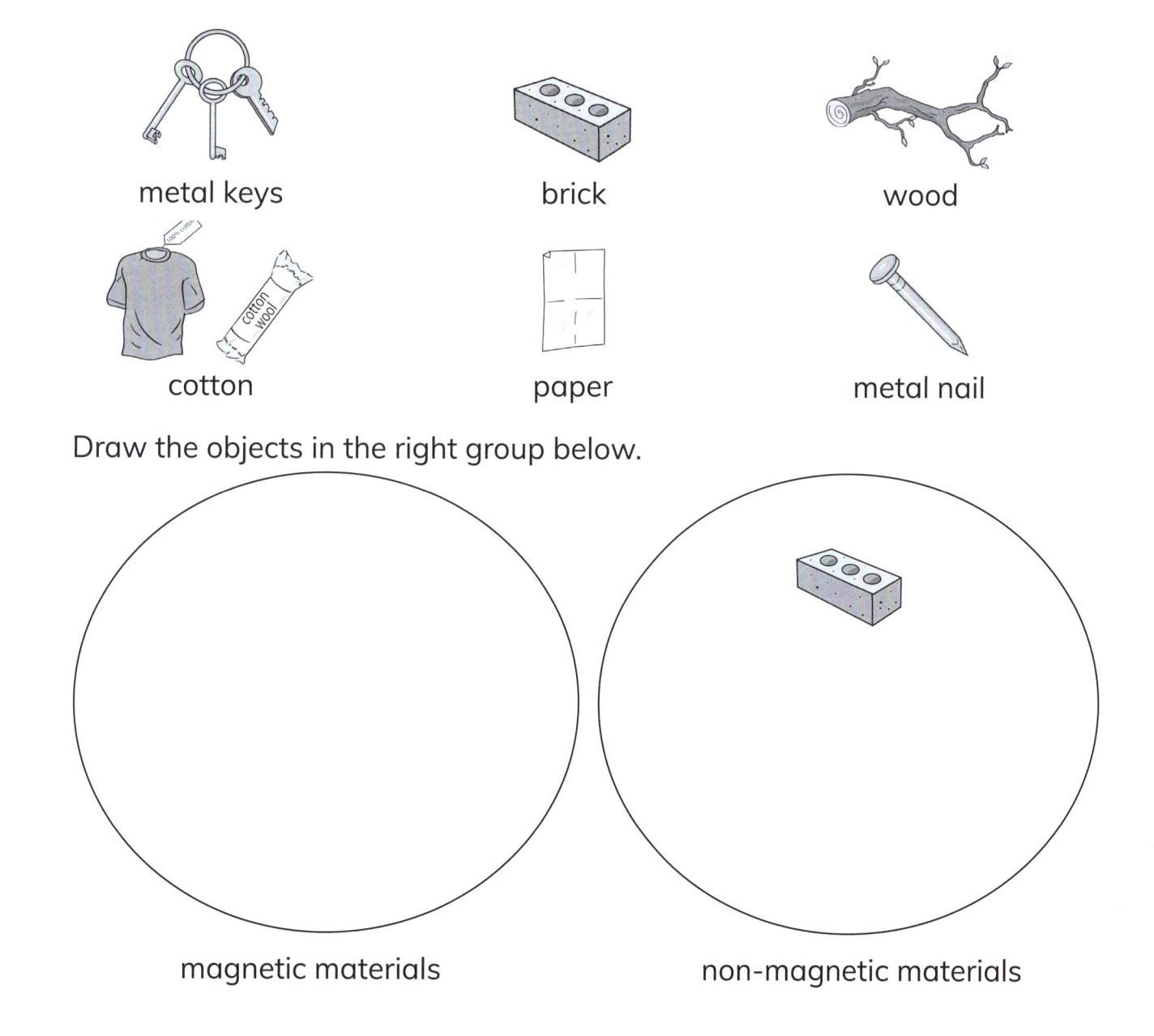

   metal keys

   brick

   wood

   cotton

   paper

   metal nail

   Draw the objects in the right group below.

   magnetic materials

   non-magnetic materials

6 Forces

Practice

2 Depal tests materials with a magnet.

Complete his table.

Draw a circle around the correct word in each case.

Object	Material	Magnetic or non-magnetic
	wood	magnetic / (non-magnetic)
	metal	magnetic / non-magnetic
	plastic	magnetic / non-magnetic
	paper	magnetic / non-magnetic
	metal	magnetic / non-magnetic

3 Draw a circle around the material that is magnetic.

paper   metal   wood   plastic

6.5 Magnets can pull

Challenge

4 Magnets pull magnetic materials towards them.

Look at the pictures. Some materials are magnetic and other materials are non-magnetic.

Draw arrows to show the pulling force on the magnetic materials.

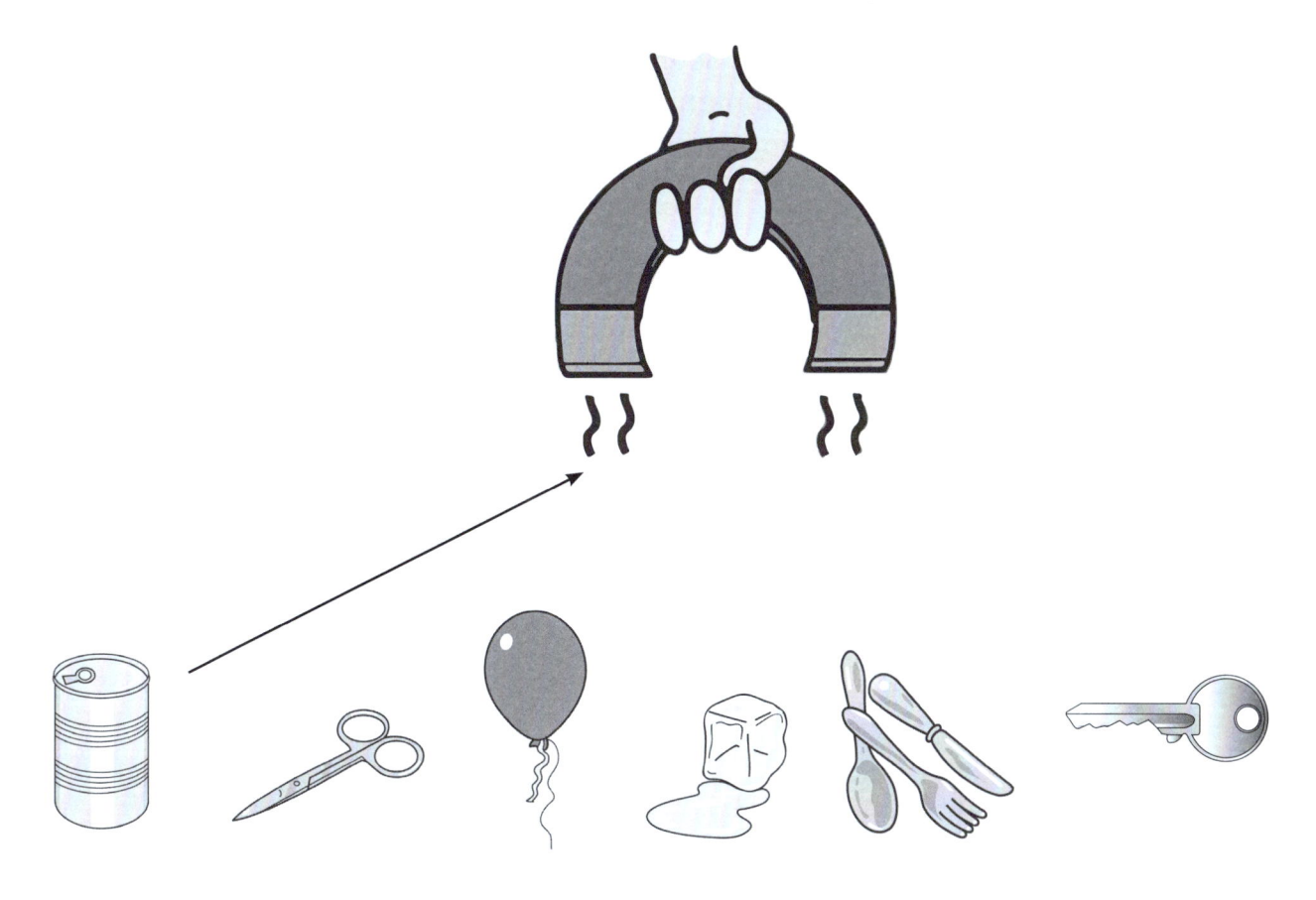

Why does the magnet not pull on the rubber balloon?

_____

_____

_____

79

Acknowledgements

Thanks to the following for permission to reproduce images:

Cover illustration by Omar Aranda (Beehive Illustration); *Inside Unit 1* TravelCouples/Getty Images; Image Source/Getty Images; *Unit 3 Dale Hauer/ EyeEm/Getty Images; Unit 4 frenchman77/Getty Images; R.Tsubin/Getty Images; Unit 5 Catherine Falls Commercial/Getty Images; Unit 6 Robert Christopher/* Getty Images